A MOUNTAIN B
TO THE HIGHWAYS AND BRIDLEWAYS OF
HAMPSHIRE AND
THE NEW FOREST

1st edition published August 1995

ISBN 1-898073-07-4

© Power Publications
1 Clayford Ave
Ferndown, Dorset.

ACKNOWLEDGMENTS
In researching this collection of cycle rides we would like to thank
Anna and John Whitehouse for their perserverance in researching
three of the rides in extreme 'February' weather. We are grateful to
my parents, Derek and Evelyn Hancock, and to Mike Power for
undertaking some of the route research in the New Forest.

PUBLISHER'S NOTE
Whilst every care has been taken to ensure the accuracy of all the
information given in this book neither the author nor the publisher
can accept responsibility for any mistakes that may occur.

PRINTED BY: ALRESFORD PRESS LTD
BOOK PHOTOS: BONITA TOMS AND MIKE POWER.
DESIGN: GRAHAM WHITEMAN.
MAP DRAWINGS: MIKE POWER
FRONT COVER: BONITA TOMS

CONTENTS

INTRODUCTION

Hampshire is blessed with a diverse and interesting landscape, from the rolling chalk downland of the northern hills and the tranquil unspoilt river valleys, etched by the delightful clear chalk streams of the Test, Itchen, Avon and Meon, to the fascinating and beautiful medieval forest and heathland of the New Forest.

Despite having its fair share of busy main roads, motorways and ever sprawling towns, Hampshire offers a wealth of traffic-free country lanes, bridleways and byways, which link charming thatched and timbered villages and peaceful open countryside - ideal for those keen to escape the rat race.

Other than walking, the best way to appreciate Hampshire's beauty is to explore

this enviable network of highways and byways on a bike. Cycling is not only great fun, it is a major ingredient for a healthy life, as it increases your level of fitness by exercising both your heart and lungs, as well as improving stamina levels, generating a hearty appetite and relieving the stresses and strains of modern-day living.

In a society ruled by the motor vehicle and its related unhealthy consequences, cycling is a harmless and an environmentally-friendly way to explore the countryside. Unlike walking, cycling gives you more freedom to roam. Greater distances can be covered on a bike, yet the activity still brings you into intimate contact with the sights, sounds and smells that exist around you, while freewheeling through picturesque landscapes.

This selection of 30 cycle rides delves deep into the heart of the New Forest and across Hampshire, transporting the cyclist through some of the best countryside and historic villages that this magnificent county has to offer. All the rides are circular, varying in length and difficulty, from easy all-road routes to more challenging circuits with often testing off-road sections. Distances range from 11.5 miles (18.5km) to 26 miles (42km). My aim in researching and producing a varied choice of routes is to appeal to all cycling abilities, from novices and family groups to more experienced off-road bikers. More adventurous cyclists can easily link two routes for more extensive and challenging day tours, incorporating significant track riding. Note: it is recommended that you purchase the appropriate Ordnance Survey map for each route, as these show all the permitted tracks and bridleways, and provide more detail than the sketch map provided for each ride.

It is advisable on most of these rides to use a mountain bike, or a sturdy hybrid cycle, as the tracks and bridleways can often

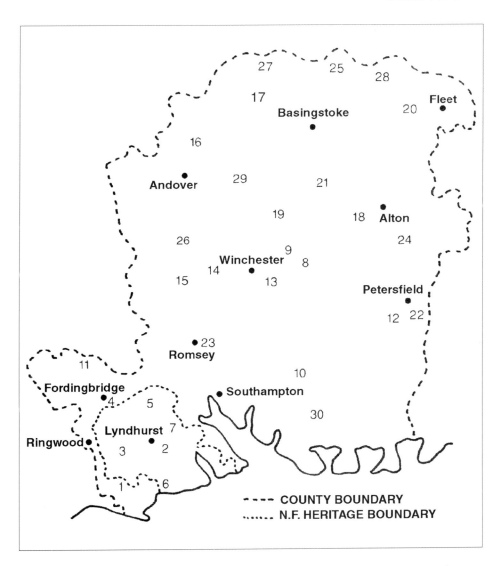

27   25   28

17
Basingstoke
20   **Fleet**

16

Andover   29   21

19   18 **Alton**

26   24

9
Winchester 8
14   13

15

Petersfield

12 22

• 23
Romsey

10

11
Fordingbridge
4   5   **Southampton**
30

Lyndhurst 7
Ringwood
3   2

1   6

- - - - **COUNTY BOUNDARY**
.... **N.F. HERITAGE BOUNDARY**

be rutted, muddy and very wet, especially during the winter months - exactly the season and conditions I experienced during the research of this guide! However, during the drier summer months conditions on many of the off-road stretches should be suitable for all types of bikes, if ridden with care.

No approximate time for the completion of each ride is given, as it is very difficult to assess. Cycling ability, inclement weather, number of hills, conditions of the off-road tracks, pub visits and stops 'along the way' to explore villages and sights will all affect the time taken to finish a route. Remember - this guide is primarily aimed at the leisure cyclist wishing to savour Hampshire's countryside and heritage, rather than an oblivious, head-down blast through the lanes!

ESSENTIAL INFORMATION

ROUTE DETAILS

Each of the rides featured in this guide are circular and range from 11½ miles (18.5km) to 26 miles (42km) in length, with total distances varying according to difficulty and the amount of off-road cycling involved. Some of the routes are relatively easy all-road circuits, others are more demanding rides incorporating tracks and byways, the off-road distance being stated after the total distance of the ride. The hilly nature of the terrain and the degree of difficulty of each ride can be easily assessed by referring to the boxes on the map and the corresponding key on page no 9. It is important to remember that cycling off-road will vary in difficulty depending on the season. Prolonged wet weather and general winter conditions will find most bridleways churned with mud and awkward to negotiate on a bike, classifying it as 'difficult'. During the summer months tracks are usually hard and dry and thus become relatively 'easy' to ride on.

An introductory paragraph 'sets the scene' for each route, highlighting the type of area and terrain to be covered, noting any particularly difficult off-road sections and features the interesting diversions along the way, such as villages and places to visit.

I have generally assumed that most cyclists will be using a vehicle to transport their bikes to the start point. Each ride therefore starts and finishes from a designated village or rural car park. I have given the exact location of the start points and provided a six-figure OS grid reference to aid pin-pointing the relevant car park. For those intending to use the train to reach the beginning of the rides, I have mentioned the nearest railway station and stated its distance away from the start. In some cases a ride can be joined halfway round from a railway station. I have indicated at which point of the route this is possible. If

you intend using the train check that your bike can be transported on that route, or make sure you reserve a space for your bike, as some trains have a limited carrying capacity. It is wise to label your bike with your name and destination point.

Not every member of the family has a bike and visitors to the area may not have their cycles with them, but wish to explore the delights of the Hampshire countryside. To aid their enjoyment the nearest cycle hire centres/shops have been researched and listed, along with all the cycle shops on, or in close proximity, to each route, just in case essential spares or emergency repairs are required.

As well as the highlights, the hazards likely to be encountered on each ride are stressed, so take heed of the 'Watchout!' notes which list potential difficulties and dangers.

All the rides are designed to be leisurely half or full day outings in the countryside, so refreshment details have been listed, including pubs (bearing in mind children), tea rooms and cafés, to ensure that thirsts are quenched and energy levels are restored. I have included telephone numbers of most establishments, so that opening and food times can be checked, but if a pub is open all day it is mentioned. Many like to take a picnic with them, so suitable sites are highlighted.

The 'Along the Way' section of each ride underlines the relaxed nature of these routes. Included here are historical notes on charming villages and towns, details and opening times/telephone numbers on various historic houses, museums and gardens that are open to the public and information on country parks and wildlife. These places of interest or educational diversions allow the opportunity to explore the area out of the saddle, thus enhancing the time spent on the ride. For more information contact the relevant Tourist Information Office which is listed on page no. 9

With 30 rides across the New Forest and Hampshire, it is inevitable that some of the rides will overlap. The 'Link Information' section highlights where rides can be connected together to make a longer ride. This extends the scope of the guide, the opportunity to extend rides appealing to those cyclists with more experience and/or more energy, with the shorter rides providing ideal enjoyment for family groups and generally novice cyclists.

ON AND OFF-ROAD SAFETY

In devising this collection of cycle rides, every effort has been made to incorporate traffic-free country lanes, bridleways, byways and designated cyclepaths, usually good Forestry Commission tracks and disused railway lines. However, some relatively busy B-roads and short stretches of A-road have been used to link the quieter, more attractive routes. Remember the rules of the road:

- Do not ride two-abreast if there is a vehicle behind you and ride in single file on narrow and busy roads.

- Be alert, look and listen for traffic, especially on narrow lanes and blind bends and be extra careful when descending steep hills, as loose gravel can cause a serious accident.

- In wet weather make sure you keep a good distance between you and other riders.

- Make sure you indicate your intentions clearly.

- Finally, brush up on the Highway Code before venturing out on the road.

Off-road biking requires you to learn and adhere to a different code of conduct, as well as the Highway Code.

- Only ride where you know it is legal to do so. It is forbidden to cycle on public footpaths, marked in yellow. The only 'rights of way' open to cyclists are bridleways (blue markers) and unsurfaced tracks, known as byways, which are open to all traffic and waymarked in red. Do not cycle on private land without the permission of the owner. Note: In the New Forest keep to the gravelled Forest roads, cycling on the grass rides and unmade tracks is not permitted.

- Always yield to walkers and horses, giving adequate warning of your approach.

- Keep to the main trail to avoid any unnecessary erosion to the environment beside the paths and prevent skidding, especially if it is wet.

- Remember the Country Code: fasten all gates, guard against all risk of fire, take all litter with you, do not make any unnecessary noise, if cycling through a field of livestock take care not to scare the animals and if you cycle with your dog alongside, keep it under control.

To ensure extra safety when out cycling on or off-road, it is advisable to make sure that your bike is in good working order and equipped properly. Wear appropriate clothing and take extra clothing and a waterproof jacket with you. Ultimately, be seen by wearing bright clothing, reflective strips or sashes and make sure lights are attached to your bike if you intend cycling at night. It is advisable to wear an approved safety helmet, particularly for young children. Finally, carry sufficient food and water, a small first aid kit and enough money to purchase food and make a telephone call in case of an emergency.

BEFORE YOU GO

Having heeded the general points about cycling safety on and off the road, it is

important to consider certain factors concerning personal fitness, cycle maintainence, what to wear and necessary equipment to take with you, before you set out on a day's ride. The following notes and advice should aid your preparation.

- If you are returning from a long absence 'out of the saddle', or are relatively new to cycling, attempt the shorter rides first to develop your fitness and confidence on a bike, then tackle the longer and more challenging routes.

- Regularly service your bicycle to keep it safe and roadworthy. Check for frayed cables, worn brake blocks and tyres, broken spokes and excess play in bearings.

Inflate tyres to the correct pressure, lubricate the chain and gear mechanisms and make sure everything is firmly attached and correctly adjusted. Equip your machine with a pump, a bell, a set of lights and a rear rack.

- Comfort is the key when considering what to wear. Essential items for wellbeing on the bike are padded cycling shorts, warm stretch leggings (avoid tight-fitting and seamed trousers), stiff-soled training shoes and a good wind and waterproof jacket, ideally one made of a breathable Goretex-style fabric.

- Invest in a pair of medium-sized panniers (rucksacks are unwieldy and can affect balance) to carry the necessary equipment for a day's ride. Take with you extra items of clothing, the amount depending on the season, and always pack a light wind/waterproof jacket. Carry a basic tool kit - tyre levers, puncture outfit, adjustable spanner, screwdriver, set of Allen keys - and practical spares, such as a spare inner tube, a universal brake/gear cable and a selection of useful nuts and bolts. Remember to take a secure lock with you.

• Cycling, especially in hilly terrains and off-road, saps energy, so take adequate refreshment supplies. Consume high energy snacks like cereal bars, cake or fruit, eating little and often to combat feeling weak and tired. Plan a relaxing picnic, pub lunch or cafe stop to replenish energy levels. Always carry plenty of water, especially in hot and humid weather conditions.

TOURIST INFORMATION CENTRES

Alton	01420 88448
Andover	01264 324320
Basingstoke	01256 817618
Eastleigh	01703 641261
Fareham	01329 221342
Fleet	01252 811151
Fordingbridge (summer)	01425 654560
Lymington (summer)	01590 672422
Lyndhurst	01703 282269
Petersfield	01730 268829
Portsmouth	01705 826722
Ringwood (summer)	01425 470896
Romsey	01794 512987
Southampton	01703 221106
Winchester	01962 840500

GRADE OF RIDE INFORMATION

A guide to the degree of difficulty of each ride and the nature of the terrain to be encountered is indicated by * and $ beside each route map. However, it is important to re-emphasize that changing seasons and varying weather conditions will affect the difficulty of each ride. An extra (*) indicates that a moderate ride may become demanding in places during the winter months, when some tracks and bridleways are rendered wet and muddy and awkward to negotiate. An additional ($) indicates where a ride has only one or two testing climbs throughout a generally undemanding ride. The key to the grading is as follows:

GRADE OF RIDE

★   Easy all-road ride

★★   Moderate ride, road and good gravel tracks and grassy lanes

★★★   Demanding in places, possibility of wet and muddy tracks

★★★★ Long ride, incorporating often difficult off road riding

HILLS

$ Generally level with a few gentle inclines

$$ Rolling landscape with undemanding hills

$$$ Hilly terrain with some testing climbs and descents

$$$$ Significant hard off-road climbs and steep descents

        This symbol denotes a Public House

PEACEFUL LANES AND FOREST TRACKS BETWEEN BRANSGORE AND BURLEY

13½ miles (21½ km) / 5½ miles (8.8km) off-road

OS Maps

Landranger 195 (Bournemouth and Purbeck) 150,000.
Outdoor Leisure 22 (New Forest) 1:25,000.

Nearest Railway Station

Hinton Admiral, 2½ miles (4km) south.

Cycle Shops/Hire

Burley Bike Hire, Burley
☎ 01425 672088.
Ashley Cycles, 49 Ashley Road, New Milton ☎ 01425 72347.

Watchout!

- when crossing the A35 twice.

Link Information

Explore this area of the Forest further by joining the Burley ride (route 3), either at point 2 along the old railway line or from the start of the ride two-thirds of the way round this route.

Refreshments

Bransgore - Three Tuns (16th-century/good bar food/large garden/children welcome)
☎ 01425 72232.
Crown Inn (open all day/popular family venue - play area)
☎ 01425 672279.

Burley - Queens Head
☎ 01425 403423.
Several tea rooms.

Picnic along the Inclosure tracks or at the designated picnic area on Wilverley Plain.

A short easy ride on traffic-free rural lanes and well surfaced Inclosure and heathland tracks from the small Forest-fringe village of Bransgore. The ride incorporates the traditional Forest village of Burley, a welcoming resting place in which to enjoy an afternoon tea, and the more adventurous cyclist can extend the ride into the New Forest by linking with the Burley ride.

START

Bransgore. Small village located on the edge of the New Forest, signposted off the A35 Christchurch to Lyndhurst road, 1½ miles (2.4km) north east of Christchurch. Free car park situated behind the main shopping parade. OS grid ref: SZ190977.

ROUTE DIRECTIONS

1. From the car park turn left into the lane and go straight across the crossroads to cycle along Ringwood Road. Proceed through the village, then at a left-hand bend turn left into Harrow Lane. On reaching a junction turn left, then shortly turn left again into Forest Road.

2. Cycle over the cattle grid and turn right onto the well surfaced track leading to Holmsley Campsite. At the end of the metalled track continue ahead across the grass, making for the wooden gate leading into Holmsley Inclosure (can be locked to keep ponies out at certain times, so lift bike over). Follow the dirt track ahead down through the trees, turning right onto the wide gravel track at the bottom and out through the wooden gate into a lane. Turn right and cycle uphill to reach the A35.

3. Turn left, then immediately right through a gate onto a gravel track and proceed ahead to a second gate to enter Brownhill Inclosure. Shortly, fork left, then after rounding a right-hand bend take the dirt track on your left, down to join a gravel track and turn right. Disregard the side turnings off the track and keep to the main track

as it twists and turns through attractive mixed woodland, finally reaching a gate and lane and turn left.

4. Cross the bridge, cycle up to the T-junction (just before it bears off right beside a barrier and shortly join the old railway track and the Burley ride) and go straight across onto the gravel track, soon to leave by the narrow path to the right. Cycle up the road (can be busy) until you reach the chevron signs on the left, then turn left along the grass track and through the parking area. Continue along a gravel track, cycling past Wilverley Plain, with The Naked Man - actually an old tree - on your right. Eventually reach a gate and the main A35.

5. Carefully cross this busy road, pass through a gate onto a further track and continue cycling along this old road to reach a metalled drive. At a road junction turn left, then right and pedal down into the picturesque village of Burley. Turn left and left again by the war memorial onto the Bransgore Road (also the beginning of the Burley ride), cycling the 4 miles (6.4km) across open forest and through Thorny Hill (note the unusual church) back into Bransgore.

ALONG THE WAY

Burley
Traditional New Forest village surrounded by colourful heathlands and oak, beech and pine woodland. Ponies, donkeys and cattle still roam freely in the pretty village centre, which has become a very popular destination with visitors to the Forest. 'Bur' comes from the Anglo Saxon word 'Burgh' meaning hill or fort and close to the village is Castle Hill, which rises to 300ft and is crowned with ditches and banks of an Iron Age hill-fort. The Queens Head pub displays a fine collection of weapons and hunting trophies.

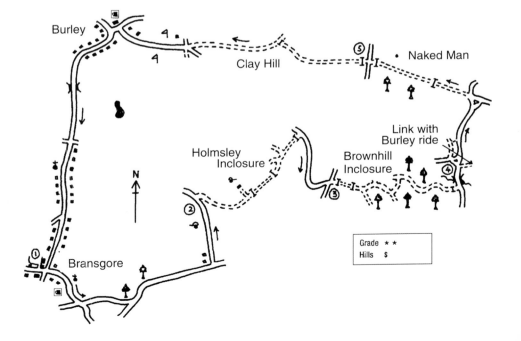

Grade ★ ★
Hills $

INCLOSURE AND HEATHLAND TRAILS AND FOREST FRINGE LANES FROM BROCKENHURST

20 miles (32km) / 11½ miles (18.4km) off-road

OS Maps

Landranger 196 (Solent and the Isle of Wight) 1:50,000. Outdoor Leisure 22 (New Forest) 1:25,000.

Nearest Railway Station

Brockenhurst.

Cycle Shops/Hire

New Forest Cycling Experience (hire/spares), Brockley Road, Brockenhurst ☎ 01590 24204.
Active Cycles, South Street Centre, Hythe ☎ 01703 843396.
Cycle World, Commercial Road, Totton ☎ 01703 660829.
Strides Cycles, Commercial Road, Totton ☎ 01703 873383.

Watchout!

- when descending the loose gravel tracks.
- on the B3054 at Beaulieu, it is quite busy especially during the summer months.
- when crossing the often boggy Matley Heath.

Link Information

It is possible to link this ride with three other Forest rides: just before Beaulieu (point 2) follow signs to Bucklers Hard to join the Lymington ride (route 6, point 3/all-road); just prior to the railway line and Matley Heath (point 4) turn right into Deerleap Inclosure to link with the Lyndhurst ride (route 7, point 2) and extend your ride from Brockenhurst by incorporating the Burley ride (route 3, point 3).

A most enjoyable Forest ride that explores excellent gravel tracks through tranquil inclosures and heathland lanes, as well visiting the historic village of Beaulieu with its palace and National Motor Museum. A short diversion offers the opportunity to visit the charming riverside village of Bucklers Hard. Off-road sections are generally dry, except the earth tracks across Matley Heath and Matley Wood, which can be very wet in winter.

START

Brockenhurst. Park in the free car park at the junction of the A377 Lyndhurst to Lymington road and the B3055 to Beaulieu, just north of the village at Balmer Lawn.
OS grid ref: SU303031.

ROUTE DIRECTIONS

1. Turn right out of the car park onto the B3055 and pass through Balmer Lawn. In ¼ mile (0.4km) bear off left onto a gravel track, signed car park. Cross heathland, pass Tillery Road car park and soon bear left to reach Standing Hat car park. Keep right beside a barrier, then go through a gate, passing behind a Forest cottage. Enter Perrywood Haseley Inclosure and disregard all routes off the main gravel track until reaching a crossing of tracks (D12 post). Turn right, pass through a gate, then cross the railway bridge and in 150 yards turn left through a gate into a deer research area.

2. In just over ½ mile (0.8km) at a crossing of five routes, turn right (deer research post) and gently ascend to a gate. Bear left to a further gate, descend to a crossing of tracks and turn left, then keep left uphill where tracks merge. Soon descend the gravel track to cross a brook and leave the inclosure via a gate. Proceed uphill across heathland, pass beside a barrier and soon bear right onto a metalled track by a group of cottages, eventually

reaching the junction of the B3055 and B3054 at Hatchet Pond. Turn left and take care as you cycle for a mile (1.6km) into Beaulieu. Turn right to visit the village. If wishing to visit Bucklers Hard (2 miles/3.2km), or join Lymington route, turn right just before Beaulieu, signed Bucklers Hard.

3. Continue on the B-road (now B3056), passing the entrance to the National Motor Museum/Beaulieu Abbey, then in ½ mile (0.8km) take the first turning right and cross the Beaulieu River. Cycle along this generally level road through woodland and across open heathland for 2½ miles (4km), soon to leave the Forest boundary via a cattle grid. Pass the Bold Forester pub and turn left, signed Colbury and continue for 1½ miles (2.4km) along this quiet lane, before turning left into Deerleap car park, located just beyond the tourist sign for Longdown Dairy

Refreshments

Brockenhurst - range of pubs and tea rooms.

Beaulieu - Wine Press (Montagu Arms) (open all day summer) ☎ 01590 612324.
Old Bakehouse Tea Rooms. Restaurant/cafe in National Motor Museum (access only if visiting palace and museum).

Marchwood - Bold Forester (children welcome/play area/carvery-style food) ☎ 01703 865967.

Longdown - New Forest Butterfly Farm (picnic area/restaurant) ☎ 01703 292166.

Take a picnic and enjoy it beside one of the Forest tracks.

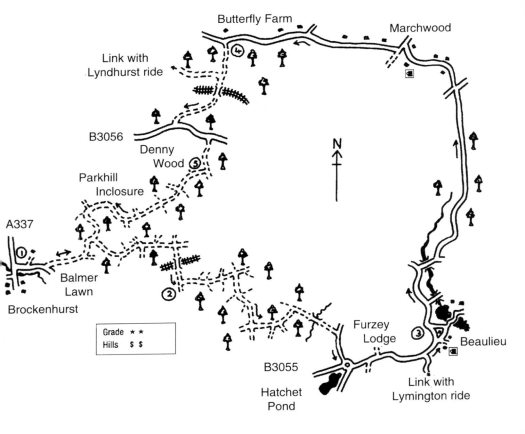

Farm. The New Forest Butterfly Farm is situated a short way along the lane.

4. Cross the car park, pass beside a barrier and proceed on a good heathland track between inclosures to a group of pine trees near the railway. (Turn right here through a gate into Deerleap Inclosure to link with the Lyndhurst ride). Cross the railway bridge and the Beaulieu River, then head across Matley Heath, keeping right of the small lake, and enter Matley Wood. Shortly, cross a track and pass through Matley Heath Campsite/parking area, passing beside barriers, to reach the B3056. Turn left, then in ¼ mile (0.4km) bear off right at a sharp left-hand bend into the access road to Denny Wood Campsite.

5. Keep to the metalled track through the site, then on reaching the private entrance to Denny Lodge, bear off right (D8 sign) onto a gravel track through Denny Wood. Remain on this trail, ignoring all routes left and right, then in about ¾ mile (1.2km) keep left, then in 100 yards keep right at a junction, soon to curve sharp right into Parkhill Inclosure. At the next junction (D3 sign) turn left and follow it sharp left as it gently undulates through the Forest. At a junction of five routes (D2 sign), keep to the main track which curves left, then right downhill (care), eventually reaching a gate and Standing Hat car park. Retrace your outward route back to Balmer Lawn and the car park.

RAILWAY AND FOREST TRACKS BETWEEN BURLEY AND BROCKENHURST

19½ miles (31.5km) / 11½ miles (18½km) off road

OS Maps

Landranger 195 (Bournemouth and Purbeck) and 196 (Solent and the Isle of Wight) 1:50,000. Outdoor Leisure 22 (New Forest) 1:25,000.

Nearest Railway Station

Brockenhurst (mid-point of ride).

Cycle Shop/Hire

Burley Bike Hire, Burley
☎ 01425 672088.
New Forest Cycling Experience, Brockley Road Brockenhurst
☎ 01590 24204.

Watchout!

 - for the height barrier at the car park entrance if carrying bikes on the roof.
- on descending some of the loose gravel tracks.
- on crossing the straight and fast section of the A35.

Link Information

This route joins the Brockenhurst ride (route 2, point 1) and an additional loop incorporating the Bransgore ride (route 1, point 4) can be ridden from Burley. An extended Forest tour can be enjoyed by diverting for 2½ miles (4km) to link with the Fritham ride (route 5, point 4).

A fairly lengthy, but level ride using predominantly good gravel tracks between the popular Forest villages of Burley and Brockenhurst. From Burley the route follows a delightful old railway route across open heathland, returning through peaceful forest inclosures and along a section of the attractive Bolderwood Ornamental Drive. Excellent picnic opportunities, or allow time for lunch or tea in Brockenhurst, the mid-way point.

START

Burley. Popular tourist village situated on the western fringe of the New Forest, signposted off the A31, 3 miles (4.8km) east of Ringwood. Free car park located behind the Queens Head pub in the village centre.
OS grid ref: SU211031.

ROUTE DIRECTIONS

1. Turn right on leaving the car park and keep right at the junction by the Queens Head into the village centre. In 50 yards, bear left for Bransgore and follow Pound Lane out of the village. In a mile (1.6km) turn left into Burbush Hill car park and keep left along a defined track to join the course of the old Southampton to Dorchester railway track. Remain on this splendid level and well surfaced trail for 2 miles (3.2km) to a stile beyond an old platform. Carry your bike over the stile to reach a road opposite the Old Station Tea Rooms.

2. Turn left, then right at the T-junction, signposted Sway. Proceed for 1 mile (1.6km) - can be busy - along a straight road, then where it bears left, turn right for New Milton. In 20 yards, bear left beside a wooden barrier and follow a grassy track left to rejoin the disused railway trail. Continue for a further 2 miles (3.2km), passing through Setthorns Campsite, eventually reaching a track by some cottages. Bear right and shortly reach the B3055.

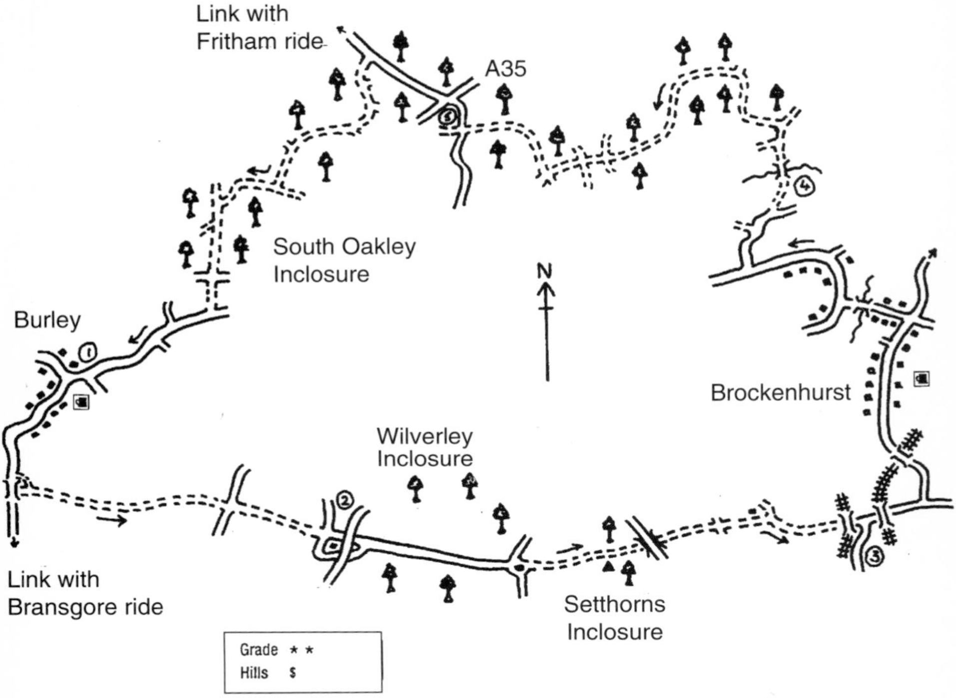

Link with
Fritham ride

A35

South Oakley
Inclosure

Burley

N

Brockenhurst

Wilverley
Inclosure

Link with
Bransgore ride

Setthorns
Inclosure

Grade ★ ★
Hills $

Refreshments

Burley - Queens Head ☎ 01425 403423, Burley Manor Hotel (coffee & teas) ☎ 01425 403522, and various tea rooms, including the Old Station Tea Room midway between Burley and Brockenhurst.

Brockenhurst - numerous pubs and tea rooms, notably Thatched Cottage Hotel ☎ 01590 23090 and Forest Park Hotel ☎ 01590 22844.

ALONG THE WAY

Burley
Traditional New Forest village surrounded by colourful heathlands and oak, beech and pine woodland. Ponies, donkeys and cattle still roam

3. Turn left and take the next left, to follow the B3055 for a mile (1.6km) into the centre of Brockenhurst. At a crossroads keep ahead to link with the Brockenhurst ride at Balmer Lawn on the A337, otherwise follow the main route left through the village centre, go through the shallow ford (or cross the footbridge) and turn right at the T-junction, signed Rhinefield. Pass Forest Park Hotel, then on reaching open heathland (Whitefield Moor), turn right into Beachern Wood parking area. (If wishing to cycle the beautiful Rhinefield Ornamental Drive, keep to the road - can be busy - and pick the route up near the A35). Proceed along the ramped metalled lane, pass the entrance to Aldridge Hill Campsite, then where it veers sharp right at Obers Corner Walkers car park, keep straight on along a good gravel track.

4. Shortly, cross Bolderford Bridge over the Lymington River, go through a gate and turn first left to a further gate. Follow the forest track through New Park Plantation, pass through a gate, then keep left at a

junction to another gate and enter a Wildlife Conservation Area. Remain on this track, ignoring gravel tracks right to a gate. Continue ahead, cross a stream and proceed across heathland to a gate and enter Poundhill Inclosure. Turn right at the third crossing of tracks and follow this track as it curves right, then left to reach the Rhinefield Ornamental Drive.

5. Turn right, cross with care the fast and busy A35 and continue along Bolderwood Ornamental Drive. After a mile (1.6km) just beyond Barrow Moor Picnic Area, turn left onto a gravel track, passing beside a wooden barrier. (Remain on the Ornamental Drive for 2½ miles (4km) and pass beneath the A31 to link with the Fritham ride). At a fork of tracks keep right and pass through Anderwood Inclosure. Remain on this forest track, eventually passing through two wooden gates and descend to a junction of tracks. Keep ahead (B6 marker), then bear left at the next junction, soon to cross a stream and gradually climb to a crossing of tracks. Turn right, pass a cottage, then keep left at a T-junction and follow this good track over a metalled track, via wooden barriers, finally reaching a gate and a road. Turn right then after a mile (1.6km) enter Burley with the car park located on your right.

freely in the pretty village centre, which has become a very popular destination with visitors to the Forest. 'Bur' comes from the Anglo Saxon word 'Burgh' meaning hill or fort and close to the village is Castle Hill, which rises to 300ft and is crowned with ditches and banks of an Iron Age hill-fort. It affords good views over the village and surrounding Forest. The Queens Head pub displays a fine collection of weapons and hunting trophies.

Brockenhurst
Bustling residential village in the heart of the Forest and an ideal base from which to explore the area. The Norman church is thought to be the oldest in the New Forest and the churchyard boasts an enormous yew tree which is said to be over 1,000-years-old. Buried in the churchyard is 'Brusher' Mills, a famous Forest character, who in the late 19th-century lived in a hut deep in the Forest for thirty years, making his living by catching adders, some of which he sent to zoos. His gravestone shows him with his hut and snakes.

Plains and Inclosures
The Forest abounds in wildlife, so lookout for roaming ponies on the open heathlands and deer - Fallow and Roe - grazing along the grassy forest tracks. Foxes and badgers can be seen, as well as green woodpeckers, kestrels, owls and numerous species of warblers and small woodland birds.

The Queens Head in the traditional Forest village of Burley.

AVON VALLEY LANES AND NEW FOREST HEATHLAND TRACKS FROM FORDINGBRIDGE

14 miles (22.4km) / 4 miles (6.4km) off-road

OS Maps

Landranger 195 (Bournemouth and Purbeck) 1:50,000. Outdoor Leisure 22 (New Forest) 1:25,000.

Nearest Railway Station

Salisbury, 9 miles (14.5km) north.

Cycle Shops/Hire

Sandy Balls Cycle Centre, Godshill, 2 miles (3.2km) east of Fordingbridge ☎ 01425 655002. Perkins, Fordingbridge ☎ 01425 653475. Ibsley Bike Hire, Ibsley ☎ 01425 473373. Hay Ball & Co, Salisbury ☎ 01722 411378.

Watchout!

- on the short section of main road at Ibsley - it has a very dangerous bend.

Link Information:

To explore the Forest further, link with the Fritham ride (route 5, point 2)

Refreshments

Fordingbridge - various pubs and cafés in the town.

Ibsley - Old Beams Inn (tardis-like thatched inn/notable buffet-style food/good real ales/children welcome) ☎ 01425 473387.

Linwood - Red Shoot Inn (open all day in summer/children welcome) ☎ 01425 475792. High Corner Inn (set in the Forest -excellent family facilities/food/play area) ☎ 01425 473973.

Frogham - Foresters Arms (traditional local/good real ales /children welcome) ☎ 01425 652294.

*F*rom Fordingbridge a steady road climb preceeds a gradual descent into the Avon Valley and the hamlet of Harbridge. After leaving Ibsley the route through Mockbeggar takes you along peaceful Forest roads and high up onto open, scenic heathland, returning through Ogdens and the small village of Frogham. During exceptional wet winters some of the Avon Valley roads may become flooded and difficult to negotiate, if wishing to keep your feet dry!

START

Fordingbridge. Small town located on the A338 between Ringwood and Salisbury, 5 miles (8km) north of Ringwood. Free car park signposted off the A338 in the town centre. OS grid ref: SU148143.

ROUTE DIRECTIONS

1. Turn right from the car park, entering Fordingbridge over the River Avon and fork left, then left again at the next junction. The route passes through an attractive area before climbing steadily away from the town. At the top of the hill turn left, signposted Somerley, and proceed along this peaceful country lane, turning left again when you reach the turning for Ibsley.

2. The gradual descent into the hamlet of Harbridge affords some delightful views across the Avon Valley. Pass through the village, cross the water meadows and make a right turn along the main road - (A338). Carefully make your way past the Old Beams pub, soon to turn left into Mockbeggar Road and then turn right when you reach the village of Mockbeggar. Cycle past Moyles Court School, go through the ford, or cross the footbridge, and turn left. The winding Forest road passes through an attractive area of open heathland (Rockford Common) before reaching the Red Shoot Inn, a good refreshment stop.

3. Steadily climb through mature holly trees and enter open forest. (At a sharp left-hand bend, bear off right to join the Fritham ride). Pass Broomy Walk car park on your right, then turn left onto a track leading to the High Corner Inn. Ride past the pub, bearing right along the gravel track and soon fork right at the bottom through Woodford Bottom car park to enter Broomy Inclosure. Leave by the wooden gate, turn left and shortly cross Splash Bridge.

4. Bear left, heading up the heath to join a larger track. Turn left and soon enter Hasley Inclosure via a gate. Take the left-hand track to the far side of the woodland, bearing left to a gate. Keep left past a group of pines on your right, following the narrow track which bears right across Forest meadow and soon descends past houses to a junction of tracks. Turn right into Ogdens car park, cross Huckletts Brook via a footbridge, and ascend to a lane at Abbots Well. Turn left and follow the lane through Frogham and Stuckton back into Fordingbridge

ALONG THE WAY

Fordingbridge
Small market town located to the north of the New Forest and noted for its fine 15th-century bridge which spans the River Avon. The much restored Church of St Mary has a 15th-century chapel, and an interesting bi-annual feature is the intricate carpet of flowers that are laid along the length of the central aisle at the end of the summer. The town is famous for its coarse fishing, particularly for pike.

Harbridge Church
Near the tap in the church grounds is a tombstone dated 1758. The epitaph says 'Here lies the mangled corpse of John Ballard of North Ashley aged 68, who's end was as rash and as untimely as the cause of it was cruel and illegal'. It is thought he was partaking in bull baiting.

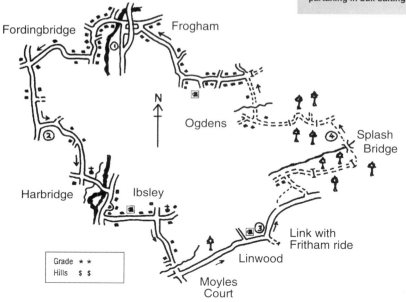

OPEN HEATHLAND AND FOREST TRACKS FROM FRITHAM

16 miles off-road

OS Maps

Landranger 195 (Bournemouth and Purbeck) 1:50,000. Outdoor Leisure 22 (New Forest) 1:25,000.

Nearest Railway Station

Lyndhurst Road (Ashurst), 8 miles (12.8 km) south east.

Cycle Shop/Hire

AA Bike Hire, Lyndhurst
☎ 01703 283349.
Burley Bike Hire ☎ 01425 672088.

Watchout!

- when descending some of the steep gravel tracks.
- many of these tracks are popular with walkers.
- for wandering ponies, cattle and pigs!

Link Information

Extend the ride by joining the Burley ride (route 3, point 5) to explore the Forest tracks further, by turning right onto the Linwood Road (point 4), pass beneath the A31 and cycle down the Bolderwood Ornamental Drive for 2 miles (3.2km). Link with the Fordingbridge ride (route 4, point 3) to venture into the Avon Valley by entering Frogham (point 2), rejoining this ride just beyond Red Shoot Inn at Roe Inclosure (point 4).

ALONG THE WAY

Fritham

Remote rural community nestling in the heart of the Forest, comprising a scattering of houses, a chapel, a farm and a thatched pub - The Royal

*T*his is an exhilarating off-road ride that explores the high open heathland and undulating Inclosure tracks that exist on the north western fringe of the New Forest. Splendid far-reaching views across the Avon Valley into Wiltshire and Dorset, an inn hidden in the Forest and delightful remote picnic spots beside brooks make this a ride to savour and enjoy. Generally good gravel tracks, but some sandy heathland trails and occasional wet and muddy areas after prolonged rain.

START

Fritham. Remote rural hamlet signposted off the B3078 between Brook and Fordingbridge, 4 miles north west of M27 J1 at Cadnam. Park in the Forestry Commission car park at the end of the village, beyond the Royal Oak pub. OS grid ref: SU231141.

ROUTE DIRECTIONS

1. If parking on the left-hand side of the car park, return towards the entrance and take the track on your left, just before the old post box. Where this track bears left keep ahead beside a wooden barrier (F6 sign) and descend on a good gravel track, soon to cross Fritham Bridge over Latchmere Brook. Ascend gradually, disregarding the gate and track to your left (F5 sign), then climb steeply to emerge out onto open heathland. With splendid open views, proceed westwards on the excellent trackway through gorse and heather, keeping left at a fork and cross Hampton Ridge.

2. Shortly, descend off the ridge to reach a metalled lane on the edge of Frogham. Bear left along the lane for the Forester's Arms if in need of refreshment, or if wishing to link with the Fordingbridge ride. The main route veers immediately left off the lane onto an uneven track 'No public access' that descends quickly to a ford and footbridge over the Latchmere Brook. Pass through Ogdens car park, then bear left at a junction of routes

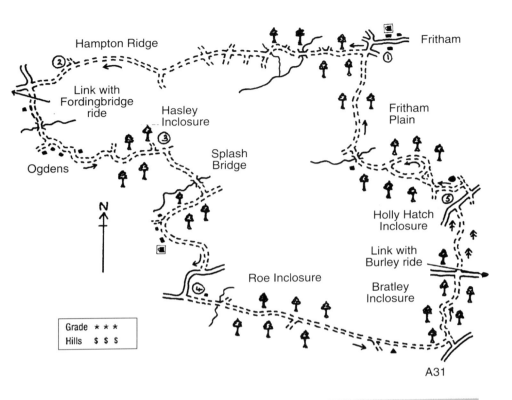

and climb gently uphill passing cottages. Follow the track left, then right beside a barrier and join a sandy track that soon bears left to gate and enter Hasley Inclosure. In a few yards keep right at a T-junction and climb around Hasley Hill to a gate.

3. Continue ahead across heathland and in 200 yards bear right along a sandy path that soon descends to a delightful secluded spot, Splash Bridge and Dockens Water. Cross the bridge, follow the track (can be muddy) beside dense coniferous woodland to a gravel forest track and go through the gate immediately on your right. After nearly ¾ mile (1.2km) pass through Woodford Bottom car park, following the access track left uphill to the High Corner Inn, nestling in the Forest and continue ascending to reach a road. Turn right, pass Broomy Walk and Amies car parks, then at a sharp right-hand bend, veer off left along a gravel track towards a house.

Oak. Many of the local people continue to exercise their ancient Forest Rights, namely letting their ponies graze the open Forest. Over 100 years ago the nearby Eyeworth Pond supplied water-power to mills used to manufacture gunpowder, the first made in England. Owned by a German the large factory employed over 100 people and was located near Eyeworth Lodge. Fritham Plain is a gorse covered heathland that is home to one the Britain's rarest heathland birds, the Dartford Warbler.

Roe Inclosure
Named after one of the species of deer that roam the vast woodlands of the New Forest. Also present in the Forest are Fallow, Red, Sika and Munjac deer, although the latter species is only occasionally seen.

Ocknell Plain
This lofty plain was an ideal choice in 1942 for one of the New Forests three main airfields. A major airbase was constructed here to aid the preparations for D-Day over 50 years ago. Although the buildings no longer stand, the present day roads follow the line of the main runways. Part of one of the runways is visible near Cadman's Pool.

Holly Hatch Cottage
Delightfully isolated between open common land and Holly Hatch Inclosure, and set beside Dockens Water, this cottage was once the home of Gilbert Smith (1906-1985). A forest keeper for many years, he also wrote the book 'Man of the Forest' which details his life at the cottage. His grandfather is supposed to have killed the last boar in the Forest.

Refreshments

Fritham - Royal Oak (limited food) ☎ 01703 812606.

Frogham - Forester's Arms (just off route/bar food/real ale/ open all day Saturday) ☎ 01425 652294.

Linwood - High Corner Inn (bar food, play area) ☎ 01425 473973. Red Shoot Inn (just off route/open all day in summer /children welcome) ☎ 01425 475792.

4. Pass through a gate into Roe Inclosure, cross Linford Brook and climb steadily to reach a gate on the woodland fringe. Head across open heathland (Bratley Plain) on a good track towards the A31. Pass a trig point, then follow the track as it curves left away from the A31, soon to reach a gate into Bratley Inclosure (L3 marker). Proceed through the wooded area to a further gate, cross a road, then pass through two more gates to continue cycling through Slufters Inclosure. (Turn right onto the road to link with Burley ride - 2½ miles/4km). Follow the undulating gravel track to a gate and shortly reach a parking area and road on Ocknell Plain.

5. Turn right, then in ¼ mile (0.4km) turn left towards a signed car park. Just before Cadmans Pool pass beside the barrier on your left to join a concrete path beside the pond. This soon gives way to a earth track leading across heathland towards Holly Hatch Inclosure. Soon go through a gate into the wood, then bear right at a crossing of tracks and curve left downhill to a T-junction of routes. Keep right and proceed downhill for ¾ mile (1.2km) to a gate beside Holly Hatch Cottage. Beyond the gate, turn right onto a gravel track, cross Dockens Water and ascend steadily to Slodens Inclosure, eventually levelling out across Fritham Plain to reach the car park in a mile (1.6km).

Picnic spot beside Dockens Water at Splash Bridge.

FOREST FRINGE TRAFFIC-FREE LANES FROM LYMINGTON

20 miles (32km) all road

OS Maps
Landranger 196 (Solent and the Isle of Wight) 1:50,000. Outdoor Leisure 22 (New Forest) 1:25,000.

Nearest Railway Station
Lymington.

Cycle Shops/Hire
The Bicycle Barn, Leagreen Farm, Christchurch Road, Downton, 3 miles (4.8km) west of Lymington
☎ 01590 644441.
Figgures Cycles, 122 High Street
☎ 01590 672002.

Link Information
Route can be linked with the Brockenhurst ride (route 2, point 2), by taking the only lane right between Bucklers Hard and East Boldre to join the B3054 at Beaulieu (point 3). Allows extensive exploration of the Forest, via plenty of off-road tracks.

Refreshments

Lymington - numerous pubs, cafés and tea rooms, notably Bluebird at Lentune, 4 Quay Street ☎ 01590 672766.

Bucklers Hard- Master Builder's House Hotel ☎ 01590 616253, Mainsail Café (Easter to October).

East Boldre - Turfcutters Arms ☎ 01590 612331.

Pilley - Fleur de Lys (good pub food/open all day/garden) ☎ 01590 672158.

Picnic - Bucklers Hard, delightful spot beside the Beaulieu River.

A level and easy ride along fairly quiet, traffic lanes on the southern fringe of the New Forest. The route follows the Solent Way, visits the charming, riverside village of Bucklers Hard and takes in the attractive church at Boldre with its H.M.S. Hood connections.

START
Lymington. Bustling little town with yacht marina located on the A337 between Cadnam and Christchurch, 12 miles south of the M27 at J1. Park in the pay and display car park by the marina in Quay Street. OS grid ref: SU330955.

ROUTE DIRECTIONS
1. Turn right from the car park and walk your cycle through the attractive cobbled street of Quay Hill to reach the junction of the High Street and Gosport Road. If you prefer to cycle, turn left from the car park, then turn right and right again to reach the above junction. Follow Gosport Road to the right and soon bear right onto the B3054, signposted Beaulieu. Shortly, bear right at the T-junction, signed Isle of Wight Ferry. Pass the ferry terminal and continue for 2 miles (3.2km) and cross a cattle grid.

2. Turn right, signposted Sowley and proceed past Sowley Pond to a T-junction. Keep right and soon pass the ruins of a chapel and a tithe barn at St Leonards Grange. At the next crossroads, turn right and follow the road for ½ mile (0.8km) to Bucklers Hard. It is well worth exploring this picturesque village, especially the Maritime Museum and riverside walk. Lock your bikes in the car park and walk through the historic village.

3. Continue along the lane and after 1½ miles (2.4km), turn left just beyond a thatched cottage, arrowed East End. (Keep ahead to link with the Brockenhurst ride). A short distance beyond the cemetery on the left, turn right for East Boldre and soon pass the Turfcutters Arms.

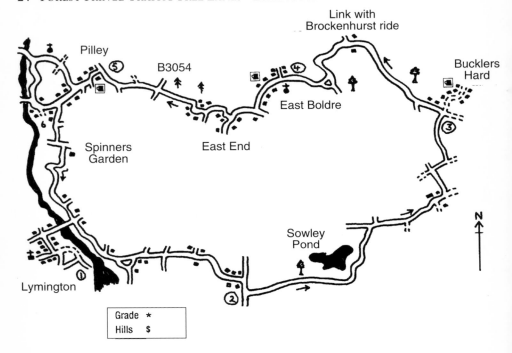

Link with
Brockenhurst ride

Pilley

Bucklers
Hard

B3054

East Boldre

Spinners
Garden

East End

N

Sowley
Pond

Lymington

Grade ★
Hills $

ALONG THE WAY

Lymington
An ancient town on the Lymington Riverwith a wide High Street, lined with 18th- and 19th-century houses.

Bucklers Hard
This small Beaulieu river village thrived for several centuries as a shipbuilding yard and Nelson's fleet were built here. A fascinating little maritime museum recalls this tradition and cottage displays recreate 18th-century life.

Boldre Church
St John's church stands isolated in the Forest,and is of interest, not only for its picturesque position, but for the memorials inside to H.M.S. Hood.

4. Skirt the edge of Beaulieu Heath, bear sharp right into East End, then in a short distance, turn right towards Norleywood and Boldre. Stay on the main route through Norleywood, then cross the B4054 into Bull Hill leading to Pilley.

5. Remain on this lane through the village, then turn right just beyond the Fleur de Lys pub (reputedly the oldest in the New Forest), into Church Lane and continue for ½ mile (0.8km) to Boldre Church (an interesting stopping place). Proceed along the narrow lane, shortly, turn left, then at a T-junction turn left and climb uphill back into Pilley.

6. Turn right, arrowed Vicars Hill and soon pass Spinners Gardens. In ¼ mile (0.4km), bear right at a junction by an oak tree and grass triangle and soon follow a narrow lane parallel with the Lymington River. At a T-junction, turn right and then right again over the causeway to retrace your outward route back into Lymington.

HEATH, FOREST AND LANE FROM LYNDHURST

13 miles (20.8km) / 4½ miles (7.2km) off-road

OS Maps
Landranger 196 (Solent and the Isle of Wight) and 195 (Bournemouth and Purbeck) 1:50,000. Outdoor Leisure 22 (New Forest) 1:25,000.

Nearest Railway Station
Lyndhurst Road Station at Ashurst, 3 miles (4.8km) north east of Lyndhurst (route can be joined here). Also Beaulieu Road Station, 1½miles (2.4km) from Matley Heath and point 2 of the ride.

Cycle Hire
A.A. Bike Hire, Fernglen, Gosport Lane, Lyndhurst
☎ 01703 283349.

Watchout!
- on the A35 at Ashurst and through Lyndhurst.
- when crossing the fast A337 south of Cadnam.

Link Information
An extended rides can be enjoyed by linking with the Brockenhurst ride (route 2, point 4) on Matley Heath.

A short and varied ride, incorporating excellent sandy heathland paths, good gravel inclosure tracks and gently undulating lanes that pass through dispersed villages on the New Forest fringe. Ideal for families, but some of the off-road paths can be muddy in winter. Minstead Church is well worth the short detour.

START

Lyndhurst. Located in the heart of the Forest on the A35 between Southampton and Christchurch. Bolton's Bench car park and picnic area is situated on the eastern edge of the town, at the junction of the A35 and B3056 to Beaulieu. OS grid ref: SU305082.

ROUTE DIRECTIONS

1. From the car park follow the narrow metalled road away from the B-road and Lyndhurst, then shortly keep right at a fork, the left-hand route arrowed to the cemetery. Join a gravel track, pass beside a wooden barrier and follow a well-defined sandy path across heathland, affording excellent views across the Forest. Keep to the main route which soon runs beside the B3056 to reach a gravel track and entrance to Matley Wood Campsite. (Proceed along the B3056 to link with the Brockenhurst ride)

2. Bear left along this track, then with the camping ground to your right soon pass beside a barrier indicating a 'car-free area'. Cycle through Matley Wood on a good track, then proceed across Matley Heath on a wide pathway. Pass a pond, then cross a stream and follow the route across a railway bridge into a group of coniferous trees. Veer off left and pass through two wooden gates into mixed woodland (Deerleap Inclosure).

3. Head immediately left at the fork of tracks, following the gravel track to a further fork. Keep left, pass through a gate and re-cross the railway. At the end of the railings

turn sharp right onto a narrow path through trees, across a small bridge and then cycle parallel with the railway to enter Ashurst Campsite. Leave via the main entrance, turn right (with care) onto the A35 and enter Ashurst.

4. In 200 yards pass the New Forest Hotel and Lyndhurst Road Station, then turn left, signposted Woodlands. After a mile (1.6km), turn left at a T-junction into Bartley Road. Shortly enter Bartley keeping left at the fork in front of Bartley Church. Pass through the scattered village, turning left at the next T-junction, then proceed ahead at a crossroads along Beechwood Road and in ½ mile (0.8km) reach the busy and fast A337.

5. Cross straight over, signed Minstead, then almost immediately bear off right towards London Minstead. Proceed on the lane through woodland, enter the hamlet and turn first left beside Yew Tree Cottage. At a T-junction bear right and enter Minstead opposite the Trusty Servant pub and green. To visit Minstead Church proceed straight across.

The Swan Inn at Swan Green

Lyndhurst
The capital of the New Forest and a popular tourist centre. The Victorian church features stained glass by Burne-Jones and William Morris and Alice Liddel, on whom the heroine of Alice in Wonderland was based is buried here. The story of the New Forest, including its history, traditions, character and wildlife are told through an audio-visual show and displays in the New Forest Museum.

Minstead
Set in an enclave within the Forest, this pretty village nestles in a maze of lanes and boasts a wealth of picture-postcard thatched cottages. The unusual 13th-century Church of All Saints is well worth a visit for its triple-decker pulpit, a double tier of galleries and a pew fireplace. The grave of the best known Minstead resident, Sir Arthur Conan Doyle, who created the character Sherlock Holmes, can be found in the churchyard.

6. Turn right, then immediately left (not signed) and descend into the hamlet of Newtown. Cross a ford, bear left at a fork and skirt Manor Wood to an unmarked junction. Turn left, pass a trout fishery, then in a mile (1.6km) enter Emery Down, bearing left in front of the New Forest Inn. Continue through the village to join the A35 at Swan Green. Turn left and take great care for the mile (1.2km) ride through Lyndhurst town centre, back to Bolton's Bench car park.

ALONG THE OX DROVE AND WAYFARERS WALK FROM ALRESFORD

15 miles (24km) / 8 miles (13km) off-road

OS Maps
Landranger 185 (Winchester and Basingstoke) 1:50,000.

Nearest Railway Station
Winchester 6 miles (9.6km) west.

Cycle Shop
Watts Cycles, Station Road, Alresford
☎ 01962 733145.

Watchout!
- both long-distance trails are popular with ramblers.
- bridleways are bumpy and rutted in places.

Link Information
Extend the ride in this area by joining the Avington ride (route 9, point 5) and taking short diversions to link with both the Preston Candover ride (route 21, point 1) and the Medstead ride (route 18, point 2).

*A*n undulating ride that explores the unspoilt and very rural countryside around the Candover Valley, north of the charming small town of Alresford. Splendid, well waymarked green lanes provide peaceful pedalling with scenic views. Over half the ride is off-road, and although tracks are generally good, allow plenty of time to complete the circuit.

START
The small country town of Alresford, located 6 miles (10km) east of Winchester off the A31. Park in Broad Street, alternatively, in the pay and display car park by the Watercress Line. OS grid ref: SU589327.

ROUTE DIRECTIONS
1. Proceed down Broad Street, heading north out of the town on the B3046, passing Alresford Pond and shortly enter Old Alresford. Just beyond the church, take the unsigned lane right and soon pass Upton Park Farm. In 100 yards at a sharp right-hand bend, keep straight ahead onto the waymarked Ox-Drove Way.

2. Gradually climb uphill on the established track (can be muddy), then in ½ mile (0.8km) cross a metalled lane. Continue in a north-easterly direction along the Ox-Drove, eventually passing through woodland and to the right of Upper Lanham Farm. Keep ahead along a tarmac farm track, then where this forks, proceed left (blue arrow) onto a rutted grassy track, with open rural views to a lane.

3. Turn left, then in 30 yards turn right at a T-junction and pass a transport depot on your left. Take the next left turn, signposted Upper Wield, then after ¼ mile (0.4km) at the village green, bear left for Preston Candover. Follow the narrow lane through the village, keep left after a mile (1.6km) towards Preston Candover

Refreshments

Alresford - Globe on the Lake (excellent garden and pub food) ☎ 01962 732294. (Hunters Restaurant (light lunches) ☎ 01962 732468.

Le Cresson Café (teas/coffees/light lunches) ☎ 01962 733246.

Totford - Woolpack Inn ☎ 01962 732101.

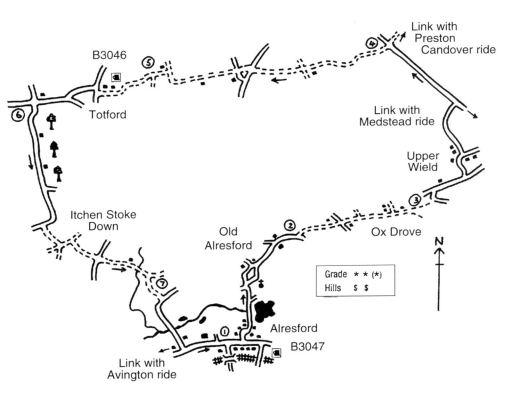

Link with
Preston
Candover ride

B3046

Totford

Link with
Medstead ride

Upper
Wield

Itchen Stoke
Down

Old
Alresford

Ox Drove

N

Grade ★ ★ (★)
Hills $ $

Alresford

B3047

Link with
Avington ride

(turn right to link with Medstead ride at Lower Wield),
then in 200 yards at a crossing of tracks, turn left with
the fingerpost to rejoin the Ox-Drove Way.

4. (If wishing to link with the Preston Candover ride
continue along the lane into Preston Candover). Back on
the main route, cycle along this delightfully peaceful
grassy track which gently undulates between open fields
and passes in front of an isolated cottage, eventually
reaching a road after 1½ miles (2.4km). Cross straight
over (waymarked), then the following narrow lane and
proceed on the wide track (Ox-Drove) to a junction of
tracks opposite farm buildings.

5. Turn left, then just beyond a black barn where the
concrete farm track bears sharp left, keep ahead to join
the Wayfarer's Walk. This often muddy and in parts
flinty track soon descends into the Candover Valley,

ALONG THE WAY

Alresford
One of Hampshire's most picturesque small towns with its wide Broad Street lined with Georgian houses and speciality shops.

Mid-Hants Railway
Also known as the Watercress Line as it was once a major despatch point for watercress. The track has been restored and is run by enthusiasts between Alton and Alresford. Steam trains run regularly during the summer and on December weekends. For timetable contact ☎ 01962 734200.

Ox-Drove
One of several ancient tracks that cross the county. Also known as 'The Lunway', it developed over time as a long-distance trade and cattle and sheep droving route linking Old Sarum to Stockbridge, then progressing north of Winchester to join the Harrow Way, east of Basingstoke to Farnham.

Wayfarer's Walk
A 70 mile long-distance trail which traverses the heart of Hampshire, linking Inkpen Beacon in the north to Emsworth on the coast in the south.

Above: A fine example of a red-brick Georgian church at Avington.

reaching the B3046 beside the Woolpack pub. Turn right, then immediately left, signposted Winchester, and soon climb out of the valley. On reaching a crossroads, turn left uphill for Itchen Abbas.

6. Continue for 1½ miles (2.4km), passing a lane arrowed to Abbotstone (splendid views across Alresford towards the South Downs), then at a right-hand bend, keep ahead to join a grassy track across Itchen Stoke Down. At a junction of five green lanes, bear slightly left and proceed straight on having rejoined the Wayfarer's Walk. Shortly, cross a lane and follow the hedged trackway that desends past a cottage and crosses the Candover Stream to a junction.

7. Keep right with the Wayfarer's Walk, then on reaching a lane turn right and cross the River Arle to reach a junction with the B3047 on the edge of Alresford. (To extend the ride, turn right for ¼ mile (0.4km) to link with the Avington ride). Otherwise, turn left for the ½ mile (0.8km) ride back into the town centre.

ALONG THE SOUTH DOWNS WAY AND THROUGH THE ITCHEN VALLEY FROM AVINGTON

19 miles (31km) / 5 miles (8km) off-road

OS Map
Landranger 185 (Winchester and
Basingstoke) 1:50,000.

Nearest Railway Station
Winchester, 5 miles (8km) west.

Cycle Shop
Watts Cycles, Station Road, Alresford
☎ 01962 733145.

Watchout!
- when crossing the A31 dual carriageway and the A272.
- for walkers on the South Downs Way.

Link Information A short diversion
along the B3047 into Alresford from
point 5 will link up with the beginning of
route of the Alresford ride (route 8).
Link with the Meon Valley ride from
Bishops Waltham (route 10, point 3) for
an extended ride south.

Refreshments

Avington - Teas on summer
Sundays and Bank Holidays in
Avington House
☎ 01962 779260.

Beauworth - Milbury's (pub food
and real ales, splendid garden)
☎ 01962 771248.

Hinton Ampner - National Trust
Tea Room, (April to September
only) ☎ 01962 771305.

Tichborne - Tichborne Arms
(good pub food and fine summer
garden) ☎ 01962 733760.

Ovington - Bush Inn (good bar
food and ales, summer garden)
☎ 01962 732764.

A quite taxing ride that climbs onto Gander Down and Millbarrow Down via the South Downs Way, affording fine rural views across central Hampshire. The return route explores the infant Itchen Valley by way of undulating narrow lanes that run close to this fine chalk stream. Refreshment can be sought at three excellent pubs around the circuit and Hinton Ampner (NT) makes a worthy resting place during the summer months.

START

Avington Park Picnic Area. Located on a minor road, 1 mile (1.6km) off the B3047 Winchester to Alresford road at Itchen Abbas, or 1½ miles (2.4km) north of the A31. From the hamlet, follow the sign for Easton to reach the picnic area beside the lake, overlooking Avington House. OS grid ref: SU528320.

ROUTE DIRECTIONS

1. Turn left out of the parking area, cross a cattle grid and shortly reach a T-junction in the hamlet of Avington. To visit the interesting church and Avington Park turn left. Our main route heads right, undulating for 1½ miles (2.4km) to reach the A31 dual carriageway. Taking extreme care, cross straight over to join a metalled farm road and gradually climb to a crossroads of tracks near a cottage.

2. Proceed ahead along a good earth bridleway - South Downs Way - and follow this rolling track with fine rural views for a mile (1.6km) to a narrow lane. Cross over, pass through a gate and ascend to the top of Gander Down and take a breather by the barn to absorb the view across the Itchen Valley. Keep to this track and descend to a gate. Continue ahead through a field, following the distinct path uphill to a further gate, then

keep to the grassy track along the left-hand edge of the field to gate. Do not go through the gate, instead bear right along the field edge and shortly pass through the gate on your left to rejoin the South Downs Way.

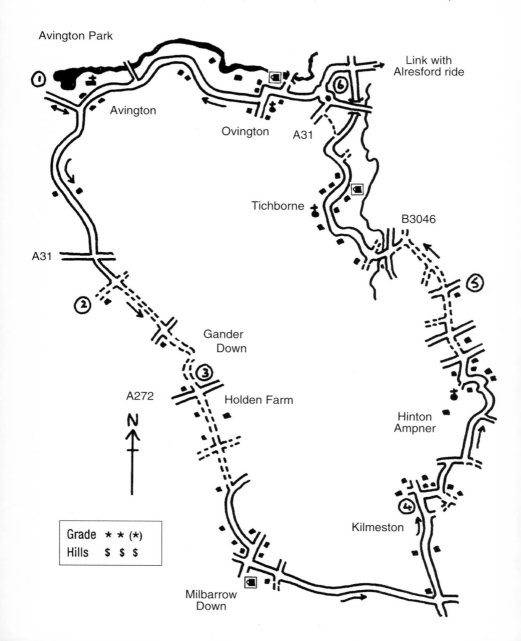

3. Cross the A272, pass through Holden Farm and follow the good trackway for ½ mile (0.8km) to a lane. Proceed straight on, uphill to a T-junction and turn right to pass the Milbury's pub. At the crossroads turn left along the ridge lane across Millbarrow Down, affording splendid views across open countryside. After 1½ miles (2.4km) turn left, signed Kilmeston and Alresford, and (turn right for ½ mile (0.8km) to Beacon Hill and link with the Bishops Waltham ride), descend on a narrow lane into Kilmeston.

4. By the village green and hall, turn right towards Dean Farm and shortly, turn left in front of Dean House. At a T-junction, bear right and pedal along this quiet lane into Hinton Ampner, passing the entrance to Hinton Ampner House (NT). Descend past thatched cottages to the A272 and cross straight over onto an arrowed by-way. Undulate on this excellent bridleway, disregarding paths left and right and soon reach a lane by a barn.

5. Keep straight on, pass a track merging from the left, then asecend to a junction of tracks. Turn left downhill to the B3046 and the Itchen Valley. Cross the B-road onto a lane, arrowed to Tichborne and shortly cross the infant River Itchen by Cheriton Mill. Follow this level lane for a mile (1.6km) and pass through the idyllic thatched village of Tichborne, including the Tichborne Arms. Proceed for 1¼ miles (2km) parallel with the Itchen to reach the B3047. (Turn right to link up with the start of the Alresford ride)

6. Turn left uphill, then take the first lane right towards Ovington and descend back into the Itchen Valley, soon to reach the Bush Inn. An interesting diversion is to follow the footpath by the car park access to a bridge over the river, a delightful spot to savour this chalk stream scene. Follow the lane uphill through the village and turn right by the telephone box, signposted Avington. Keep to this undulating valley lane with fine views to reach a junction near the entrance to Avington Park. Keep left and pass through the village, soon to turn right for Easton to return to the picnic area and car park.

ALONG THE WAY

Avington Park
A fine 17th-century mansion that boasts impressive state rooms, a library decorated with Pompeian wall paintings and a ballroom with late 17th-century ceiling paintings. Charles II stayed here and later it was bought by John Shelley, brother of the poet. Teas are served in the conservatory. Open Sunday and Bank Holidays in summer ☎ 01962 779260. In the village, the unspoilt red-brick Georgian church has box pews, a gallery and a three-decker pulpit, all supposedly made from mahogany from a Spanish Armada ship.

Hinton Ampner
Dominating the hamlet is this large 18th-century manor house, owned by the National Trust. It is noted for its landscaped gardens with terraced walks affording charming views. The small church in its grounds has a Saxon door and several handsome monuments. House and gardens open in season. Teas. ☎ 01962 771305.

Tichborne
A quaint and unspoilt thatched village nestling in the Itchen valley. St Andrew's church overlooks the village and has many interesting features, including a Norman chancel and font, Jacobean box pews and a chapel which is a rare example of a Catholic chapel situated within an Anglican church. The fascinating history notes about the village are well worth the read.

VALLEY AND DOWNLAND FROM BISHOPS WALTHAM

14 miles (20.5km) / 3 miles (4.8km) off-road

OS Map
Landranger 185 (Winchester and Basingstoke) 1:50,000.

Nearest Railway Station
Botley, 3 miles (4.8km) south west.

Cycle Shops/Hire
Bikes at Botley (repairs/hire/mobile workshop), 22 Winchester Street, Botley, 4 miles (6.4km south) ☎ 01489 790980.

Watchout!
- on the steep descent to Exton off Beacon Hill.
- when crossing the busy A32.
- for wet and muddy patches on the old railway route.

Link Information
Extend the route to explore the Itchen Valley and Alresford by making a short diversion at Beacon Hill to link with the Avington ride (route 9, point 3). Explore the Meon Valley further by joining the Wickham ride (route 30, point 2) as you leave the railway path near Soberton.

The Shoe Inn and Bridge Cottage in the delightful village of Exton.

An undulating ride mainly on little used country lanes, affording splendid views towards the Solent and the Isle of Wight, and into the beautiful Meon Valley from Beacon Hill. Picturesque valley villages and a 2 mile (3.2km) section along the dismantled Meon Valley railway line (can be muddy), make this an interesting and varied route.

START

Bishops Waltham. A small country town situated east of Eastleigh on the B2177 and 4 miles (6.4km) south west of the A32 Alton to Fareham road at Corhampton. Park in Long Lane pay and display car park, just off the B3035, near the town centre. OS grid ref: SU554175.

ROUTE DIRECTIONS

1. Turn left on leaving the car park, then at a T-junction with the B3035 turn right to leave the town. Shortly, take the first road left into Beeches Hill, signposted Cheriton and Alresford. Cross a stream, pass Northbrook Vineyard and bear off right onto a narrow lane, arrowed to Dean.

2. Proceed through the hamlet, disregarding left and right turns, then where the lane bears sharp left towards Dean Farm, turn right onto an arrowed track/drive for Franklins Farm. Pass in front of the farm, then bear left

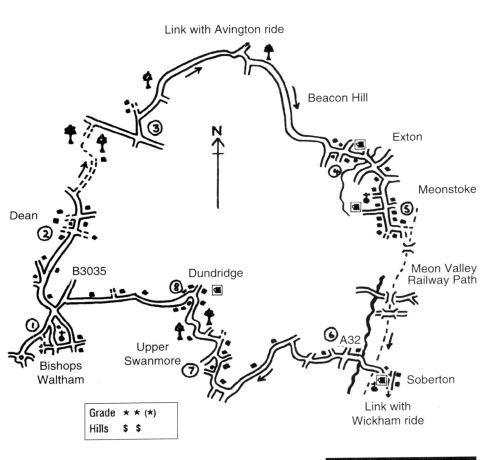

Link with Avington ride

Beacon Hill

Exton

Meonstoke

Dean

B3035

Dundridge

Meon Valley
Railway Path

Upper
Swanmore

A32

Bishops
Waltham

Soberton

Link with
Wickham ride

Grade ★ ★ (★)
Hills $ $

off the gravel drive to follow a narrow bridleway
through a line of trees. Continue between fields and
along a woodland track to a gate, then turn right along a
road for ¼ mile (0.4km) to a crossroads.

3. Turn left, signposted Kilmeston. Follow the lane past
St. Clares Farm and steadily climb uphill with unfolding
views to your right, eventually reaching a T-junction.
(Turn left to link with the Avington trail). Turn right,
then in 30 yards bear left along a lane, signed 'unsuitable
for wide vehicles'. Desend Beacon Hill (fine views) into
the Meon Valley, then beyond a sharp right-hand bend,
turn left along a lane into the village of Exton.

Refreshments

Bishops Waltham - various tea
rooms and pubs.

Exton - The Shoe Inn
☎ 01489 877526

Bucks Head - Meonstoke (open
all day in summer)
☎ 01489 877313

White Lion - Soberton
☎ 01489 877346

Hampshire Dundridge - Bowman
☎ 01489 892940

Picnic - cross a stile into fields
near Beacon Hill, magnificent
Meon Valley views.

ALONG THE WAY

Bishops Waltham
An attractive small country town with the ruins of a 12th-century palace. It was damaged in the Civil War when its Royalist defenders were defeated. The buildings have state apartments, a cloister, a great hall and a four-storeyed tower.

Meon Valley Railway
Opened in 1903 to link Alton and Fareham, it only carried passengers until 1955. Its moment of glory was in June 1944 at Droxford station, where a special train was used by the War Cabinet at the time of the D-Day landings. It is now a delightful bridleway.

Exton
An interesting collection of dwellings nestling beneath Beacon Hill with the River Meon running through its heart. Riverside scenes are best enjoyed from the small beer garden opposite the Shoe pub.

Meonstoke
Delightful village, which along with the river, are named after the Meonware tribe, who were Jutish settlers of the post Roman period. St. Andrew's church dates from the 13th-century and looks out across the idyllic river valley and attractive gardens.

4. Keep left at a T-junction, bear right by the telephone box (Shoe Inn to your left), then shortly cross the busy A32 onto an unsigned lane. Take the first lane right, then at T-junction turn right, then almost immediately left into Meonstoke. The Bucks Head pub is visible to your right.

5. Proceed through the attractive village, gradually climb uphill, then shortly bear off left along a path to join the dismantled Meon Valley Railway path. Turn right (can be muddy), following the level trail past Droxford Station, then in 1 mile (1.6km) pass beneath a bridge and climb the steps on the left up to the road. Turn right for the White Lion in Soberton if in need of refreshment, or wishing to link with the Wickham ride. Otherwise, follow the road left across the River Meon to the A32.

6. Cross over, follow the lane steadily uphill to a further crossroads and continue ahead (not signed). Keep left at an undefined T-junction, remaining on the narrow gravelly lane downhill to pass Mayhill Farm. Shortly, turn right along an unsigned lane, then at a T-junction keep right and shortly ignore the lane left, continuing through Upper Swanmore to a further junction by a post box.

7. Turn right, pass the entrance to Swanmore Park, then at a sharp right bend, veer off left onto a narrow lane and descend a 14% hill with tight bends to a junction in the hamlet of Dunbridge. With the Hampshire Bowman pub to your right, turn left signed Bishops Waltham.

8. In 1½ miles (2.4km) turn left onto the B3035 and retrace the outward route for ½ mile (0.8km) back to the car park in Bishops Waltham.

PICTURESQUE ROCKBOURNE AND DOWNLAND TRACKS FROM BREAMORE

15 miles (24km) / 8 miles (12.8km) off-road

OS Map

Landranger 184 (Salisbury and The Plain) 1:50,000.

Nearest Railway Station

Salisbury, 9 miles (14.5km) north.

Cycle Shops/Hire

Sandy Balls Cycle Centre, Godshill, 2 miles (3.2km) east of Fordingbridge ☎ 01425 655002.
Perkins, Fordingbridge ☎ 01425 653475.
Hay Ball & Co, Salisbury ☎ 01722 411378.

Watchout!

- for flooded roads along the Avon Valley during exceptionally wet winters.

Refreshments

Breamore - Bat and Ball ☎ 01725 22252. Breamore House Countryside Museum Tea Room (and toilets) ☎ 01725 512468.

Rockbourne - Rose and Thistle (idyllic thatched pub/excellent food and ale) ☎ 017235 236.

Starting from the delightful village of Breamore, with its historic house and Countryside Museum, this undulating ride takes you along attractive lanes to the pretty thatched village of Rockbourne, then after reaching Tidpit, traverses peaceful open downland on wide tracks, affording scenic views over Whitsbury. Some of the tracks can be very rutted, muddy and often flooded in winter.

START

Breamore. Sleepy village located off the A338 between Ringwood and Salisbury, 3 miles (4.8km) north of Fordingbridge. Park either in the lay-by just off the A338 or on the approach road to Upper Street.
OS grid ref: SU158180.

ROUTE DIRECTIONS

1. From the A338 take the turning signposted Whitsbury. Cycle along the lane past the open green and many delightful dwellings, then fork left past the pond and go left again at the junction. Proceed through Upper Street on a peaceful village lane and take the next turning on your right, then keep left at the bend. After a steady but gentle climb between bluebell woods, reach the brow of the hill and bear left on to the road signed Rockbourne.

2. Keep straight ahead at the crossroads, then shortly turn right to join a bridleway, waymarked Manor Farm. Pass through a gate and follow the private metalled road up to the farm. Go through a gate onto a track and climb gradually past a bluebell and primrose hedge verge to a cattle grid and enter very scenic farmland. Cycle down the metalled track to a farm gate, pass to the right of the buildings and proceed past the church to reach the village lane in Rockbourne.

3. Turn left, unless of course you are in need of refreshment, in which case the delightful thatched Rose and Thistle pub is 50 yards on the right. Pedal slowly

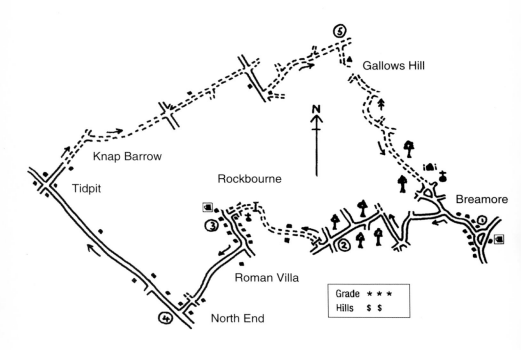

Grade ★ ★ ★
Hills $ $

through this picturesque village, then at its end turn right and proceed along an undulating road, shortly passing the turning for North End. Turn right when you reach the next junction, signposted Cranborne.

4. Cycle the length of this peaceful lane until you eventually reach Tidpit, then turn right up the narrow lane towards Toyd Down. Pedal past the farm building onto a gravel track and shortly fork right. Follow this track, deeply rutted in places and partly fenced, down to the road (can be wet in the valley) and go straight across and up the track opposite. Eventually reach a lane, turn right and cycle up the rise, soon to turn left by the tractor shed and take the track on the left across the gallop, where you may see horses from nearby Whitsbury stables being exercised. Head down into the valley, ignoring the track to the left (well rutted and often wet), then fork right until you eventually reach a signed fenced bridleway on the right.

The splended Elizabethan house a Breamore.

5. Deeply gullied, it rises onto Gallows Hill after which a narrow path enters scrub on the left, passing the trig point to rejoin the track, which bears to the right with lovely views across Whitsbury. If you wish to see the Mizmaze - a fascinating hill-top maze surrounded by yews and thought to be of a great age - divert up the bank on your right where the entrance is signed. Cycle on into the trees and fork right into Breamore bluebell woods, down past the house to the lane. Turn right for the museum and tea shop, otherwise, continue straight ahead over the crossroads back to the start point.

winding village street being lined with delightful thatched and timber-framed cottages. St Andrew's church, located on a grassy knoll, dates from the 13th-century and possesses a tiny oak shingled spire, an ornate porch and some fine memorials to the Coote family who resided nearby. The church overlooks Manor Farm, a fine complex of medieval buildings. The village is famous for its Roman Villa, discovered in 1942 and excavated during the 1950's. Open Easter to September. ☎ 017253 541.

BUTSER HILL AND THE MEONS

16 miles (26km) / 3 miles (4.8km) off-road

OS Maps
Landranger 197 (Chichester and the Downs) and 185 (Winchester and Basingstoke) 1:50,000.

Nearest Railway Station
Petersfield, 4 miles (6.4km) north east.

Cycle Hire
4 Bikes Warehouse, Horndean, 4½ miles (7.2km) south of Butser Hill off the A3 ☎ 01705 591018

Watchout!
- for the steep, often muddy and slippery descent off Butser Hill.
- on the short stretch of main road (A32) through West Meon.

Refreshments

Butser Hill - Tea kiosk

East Meon - George Inn (open all day in summer) ☎ 01730 823481

West Meon - Red Lion (open all day in summer) ☎ 01730 829264

Hambledon - Bat and Ball ☎ 01705 632692

Picnic Area - Butser Hill and Old Winchester Hill

*H*igh level lanes and tracks with magnificent views towards the Isle of Wight, contrast with pleasant meandering Meon Valley roads. Delightful East Meon is worth exploring and lingering on Butser and Old Winchester Hill will be rewarded with open downland vistas. A few steady road climbs.

START
Butser Hill pay and display car park, signposted from the A3 (T), approximately 4 miles (6.4km) south of Petersfield. OS grid ref: SU712200.

ROUTE DIRECTIONS
1. From the car park return along the access lane for 100 yards, then take the arrowed track right - Limekiln Lane - passing beside a gate and begin to descend steadily off Butser Hill. The path can be slippery in winter, but the splendid views make the slow and careful descent well worthwhile. Eventually reach a lane beside Lythe House, home to the Hampshire Wine Shippers.

2. Turn left, then on reaching a junction, bear right in front of Oxenbourne House and gently descend, following the lane into the hamlet of Frogmore. Shortly, turn right at a T-junction beside East Meon Forge and follow the High Street through the village, keeping ahead arrowed Combe where the lane bears right past the George Inn.

3. Pass the Spar shop, then bear right into Workhouse Lane, passing the village hall and a car park to a crossroads. Turn left, signposted West Meon, and cycle along the valley bottom road, parallel with the River Meon.

4. On reaching the junction with the A32, turn left and proceed with care through the village centre, soon to bear off left into Station Road. Keep to this lane and steadily ascend for 1½ miles (2.4km), with unfolding

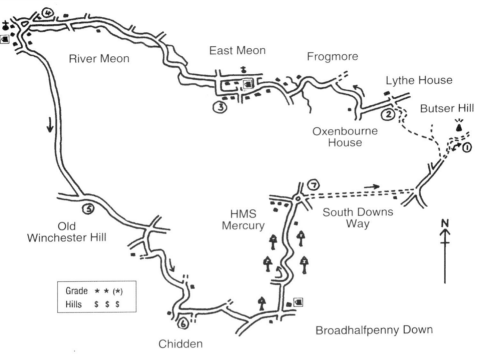

West Meon

River Meon

East Meon

Frogmore

Lythe House

Butser Hill

Oxenbourne
House

HMS
Mercury

South Downs
Way

N

Old
Winchester Hill

Grade   ★ ★ (★)
Hills $ $ $

Broadhalfpenny Down

Chidden

views, and merge with the hill-top lane. Bear left, pass
Old Winchester Hill Country Park - well worth a
breather as the views across the Meon Valley are
stunning.

5. Continue for ½ mile (0.8km) along the ridge to a
crossroads and turn right, signposted Droxford and
Corhampton. Almost immediately, keep straight ahead
at a sharp right-hand bend for Hambledon, and proceed
gradually downhill into the hamlet of Chidden. Pass
Lower Chidden Farm, then at a T-junction turn left,
arrowed Hambledon.

6. Follow a gently undulating lane to a further T-
junction, turn left, then in 200 yards, turn left again by
the Bat and Ball pub into Hyden Farm Lane. Steadily

ALONG THE WAY

East Meon

A beautiful village where Izaak Walton, the 17th-century author of 'The Compleat Angler', stayed to fish the River Meon which runs through the village centre. All Saints Church is regarded as one of the best Norman churches in the south of England, containing one of the seven black Tournai marble fonts in the country and splendid carvings.

West Meon

An attractive village noted for its associations with Thomas Lord, the first owner of Lord's cricket ground in London. He died here in 1832 and is buried in the churchyard, as is Guy Burgess, the defecting diplomat who died in Moscow.

Old Winchester Hill

It is a mystery why this noted beauty spot should be so named, as the city lies 12 miles away. The hill's windswept summit rises to nearly 700ft, affording excellent views over half the county.

Broadhalfpenny Down

The down is the site of the famous and historic cricket ground where Hambledon Cricket Club played. The club was one of the earliest to be founded in 1760, at the time when the game was played with two forked sticks as stumps. A monument to the club stands opposite the Bat and Ball pub.

Cyclists enjoying a refreshing drink at The George in East Meon.

climb uphill through woodland to a crossroads beside HMS Mercury. Turn right, then continue straight ahead at a T-junction to join the South Downs Way.

7. Follow this wide trackway across Hyden Hill and Teg Down Hill for 1½ miles (3km) to reach a metalled lane. Turn left and keep left back to Butser Hill car park.

DOWNLAND TRACKS AND LANES FROM CHEESEFOOT HEAD

16 miles (25.6 km) /5½ miles (8.8 km) off-road

OS Map

Landranger 185 (Winchester and Basingstoke) 1:50,000.

Nearest Railway Station

Winchester.

Cycle Shops/Hire

Peter Hansford (repairs/hire), 91 Olivers Battery Road South, Winchester ☎ 01962 877555 and 23a Hursley Road, Chandlers Ford ☎ 01703 266212. Peter Hargroves, 26 Jewry Street, Winchester ☎ 01962 860005. Mike's Bikes (hire), Winchester ☎ 01962 885651. Eastleigh Cycle Centre, 85 Twyford Road, Eastleigh ☎ 01703 642488.

Watchout!

- when crossing the fast and busy Morestead Road.

Link Information

Extend your ride incorporating the Avington ride (route 9, point 2) by taking the bridleway right off the A272, just below the car park.

Refreshments

Owslebury - Ship Inn (children welcome/garden) ☎ 01962 777358.

Marwell Zoo - restaurant/bar if visiting the zoo (charge).

Upham - Brushmakers Arms (real ale/good bar food/rear terrace) ☎ 01489 860231.

A short and undulating ride incorporating open downland tracks with views across Winchester, peaceful rolling country lanes and a few bridleways, which can be extremely wet and muddy after prolonged rain. Added attractions include Marwell Zoo and the charming villages of Owslebury and Upham.

START

Cheesefoot Head. Free hill-top car park located beside the A272 Winchester to Petersfield road, 3½ miles (5.6km) east of Winchester. OS grid ref: SU529278.

ROUTE DIRECTIONS

1. Turn right out of the car park, proceed for 50 yards and turn left through a green gate onto a bridleway. Keep straight on across open downland - Fawley Down - with splendid views, passing the metal flagpole, for a mile (1.6km). Pass a red-brick cottage and head downhill on a metalled track to reach the Morestead Road.

2. Taking great care, cross over into Hazeley Road and shortly take the first turning left. Descend to a crossroads and proceed straight over, signposted Owslebury. Climb steadily, bearing left at the top of the hill to pass Boyes Farm. Keep to the lane for the Ship Inn and the village, otherwise (if conditions are dry), turn right at Boyes Farm and immediately bear left onto a track, waymarked Longfield. Gradually descend, bearing left at the bottom (can be very muddy) to reach the edge of Marwell Zoo car park. Continue through the car park to the road, turn left, then at the T-junction at the end of Thompsons Lane turn right and soon reach the B2177 Bishops Waltham road. If conditions are wet it may be advisable to turn right at the roundabout by the Ship Inn in Owslebury and follow Whaddon Lane down to the B2177. (For Marwell Zoo turn right along Thompsons Lane).

ALONG THE WAY

Cheesefoot Head
The site of a great natural amphitheatre in which General Eisenhower addressed the allied troops before the D-day landings in 1944. Far-reaching views can be enjoyed across the Itchen Valley towards the hills of North Hampshire, and across the cathedral city of Winchester.

3. Turn left along the B2177, then in ½ mile (0.8km) take the first left turning, signed Roughway. Shortly, keep ahead along a track where the lane bears sharp left towards Roughway Farm. Remain on the track, which soon becomes metalled and keep left on joining the Lower Upham to Upham road. If conditions are very wet, remain on the B2177 and take the second left, opposite the Alma pub, signposted Upham. Enter Upham, pass the church, then turn left by the pond and pass the Brushmakers Arms.

4. Proceed to a T-junction and turn right, signed Winchester and Owslebury. Quickly descend White Hill and follow the lane for 1½ miles (2.4km) towards

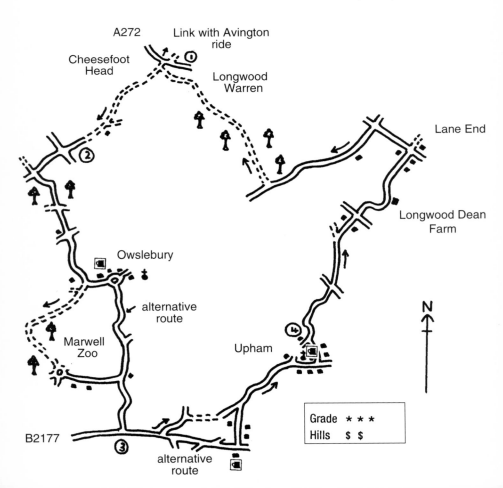

A272

Link with Avington ride

Cheesefoot Head

Longwood Warren

Lane End

Longwood Dean Farm

Owslebury

alternative route

Marwell Zoo

Upham

N

B2177

alternative route

Grade ★ ★ ★
Hills $ $

13th-century St. Andrew's Church, set in the attractive village of Owslebury.

Owslebury

A peaceful hill-top village, the second highest in the county, with a church that dates from the 13th-century, although altered on several occasions during the 17th-century. On display inside is a serpent, a primitive wind instrument used by the church band in 1840. The unusual village name is pronounced 'Ostlebury' and according to some authorities was most likely a fortified stronghold for a man called Osla.

Marwell Zoo

One of the largest zoological parks in Britain which has for the past 20 years been dedicated to the conservation of endangered animals. 100 acres of parkland surround Marwell Hall and the collection includes over 1000 animals. Open daily except Christmas Day. ☎ 01962 777406.

Upham

Interesting and unspoilt village comprising many 18th-and-19th century brick cottages and houses and a classic duck pond. Upham used to be the centre of a thriving brushmaking industry and the only surviving evidence of this is in the name of the village pub, which was once a brushmakers shop.

Longwood Dean, to reach the Winchester to Bishops Waltham road. Head straight across, then continue past Longwood Dean Farm and reach a T-junction at Lane End after 1½ miles (2.4km). Turn left, then left again at a crossroads, signed Owslebury (excellent views) and gently descend. passing the entrance to Longwood Estate. Take the second arrowed bridleway on your right, situated where the woodland meets open fields. Proceed uphill through woodland and across open farmland (Longwood Warren) on a good track, ignoring all turnings left and right, to reach the A272. Turn left back to Cheesefoot Head car park.

TRACKS AND BRIDLEWAYS AROUND FARLEY MOUNT

11½ miles (18.5km) /7 miles (11.2km) off-road

OS Map
Landranger 185 (Winchester and Basingstoke) 1:50,000.

Nearest Railway Station
Winchester.

Cycle Shops/Hire
Peter Hansford Cycles (spares/hire), 91 Oliver Battery Road South, Winchester ☎ 01962 877555. Mike's Bikes (hire), Winchester ☎ 01962 885651. Peter Hargroves Cycles, 26 Jewry Street, Winchester ☎ 01962 860005.

Watchout!
- some bridleways can be muddy and churned up.
- this area is very popular at weekends with walkers.
- for the steep and often slippery descent off Beacon Hill.

Refreshments
Sparsholt - Plough Inn (good summer garden and decent food) ☎ 01962 776353.

Farley Mount - ice cream vans on most summer days, especially at weekends.

Plenty of picnic spots in the Country Park.

*I*nvigorating off-road biking on well waymarked trails around this popular Country Park near Winchester. Good mix of woodland bridleways, little used farm lanes and open country tracks affording fine views north towards Inkpen Beacon and south west over the New Forest. Make time to visit the interesting and isolated Farley Church.

START
Farley Mount Country Park, located 2½ miles (4km) west of Winchester on Sarum Road, off Chilbolton Avenue. Park in Junction car park.
OS grid ref: SU420291.

ROUTE DIRECTIONS
1. Leave the car park and cross the unsigned junction to join a wide grassy track beyond a gate (blue arrow). Gradually descend, the bridleway narrowing through lines of scrub and trees to a junction of tracks. Turn right uphill on an excellent, yew tree-lined old green lane affording good rural views.

2. Soon bear sharp left with the main track, (private track opposite), and gently descend towards Berrydown Farm. Bear left beside the house and barn, following arrows right to join a metalled farm track. Keep right at the next junction and climb steadily uphill through trees, eventually reaching a crossroads.

3. Turn right, signed Farley Church, the metalled lane giving way after ¼ mile (0.4km), just beyond the attractive Farley Church, to a gravel farm track. Keep right through the main yard of Farley Farm and proceed along the good trackway (far reaching views west) into Parnholt Wood and a crossing of tracks. Turn right, along an often wet trackway through the woodland fringe.

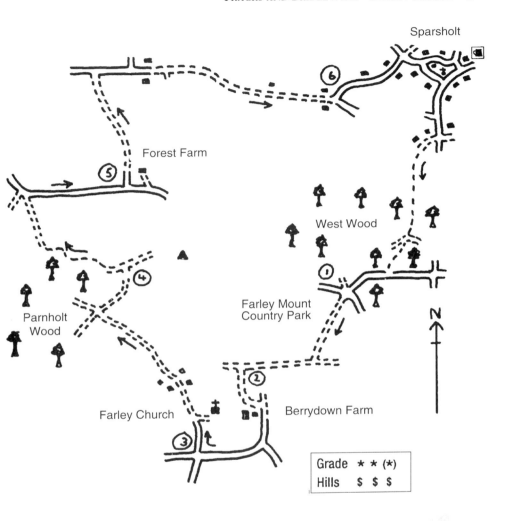

Grade ★ ★ (★)
Hills $ $ $

4. Pass beside a metal barrier and emerge out onto Beacon Hill, well worth pausing here for the splendid views. Turn left along the Clarendon Way and carefully descend off the hill on a steep, bridleway alongside woodland (can be slippery). Shortly, a good grassy track leads to a lane. Turn right along the narrow, undulating lane for ½ mile (0.8km), then turn left onto a stony track towards Forest Farm.

ALONG THE WAY

Farley Mount Country Park
Recreational area of downland and woods criss-crossed with many footpaths and trails. The best of the panoramic views offered by the stretch of open downland, are from a pyramid topping an ancient burial mound. It was built in the 18th-century in memory of a racehorse called Beware Chalk Pit, which was earned when it safely carried its rider over the unexpected hazard of a gaping chalk pit. The story is told on the memorial. The area is rich in wild flowers, notably half-a-dozen species of orchids.

Farley Church
A remote hamlet consisting of a farm, a few houses and St John's church. The latter is Norman with an old timber roof with tie-beams and king-posts and from the churchyard one can enjoy excellent views across the New Forest area.

The unusual pyramid-shaped memorial crowning Farley Mount.

5. Keep left of the farm and continue on a fenced trackway for 1½ miles (2.4km), skirting Great Up Somborne Wood to a lane. Turn right, disregard the arrowed lane left for Up Somborne, and continue along the dead-end road through a farm. Join a track, head downhill and keep ahead on merging with a track from your left and follow this valley bottom route for ¾ mile (1.2km) into Moor Court Farm.

6. At a fork, bear left steeply uphill on a metalled lane into Sparsholt. Turn right at a T-junction, then turn left along Home Lane. At a further junction, turn right to a T-junction (Plough Inn to your left), then turn right through the village centre. Pass the church, bear left, then just beyond an unsigned lane on the right, opposite Ham Green House, turn right at a crossing of tracks towards Little Sheddons. Shortly, follow a good bridleway gently uphill through West Wood to reach a lane. Turn right back to the car park.

THE TEST WAY AND CHALK TRACKS FROM HORSEBRIDGE

14½ miles (23.2km) / 6 miles (10km) off-road

OS Map
Landranger 185 (Winchester and Basingstoke) 1:50,000.

Nearest Railway Station
Romsey, 4 miles (6.4km) south.

Cycle Shops
Abbey Cycles, 70 Cherbille Street, Romsey ☎ 01794 515328. Cycle World, 109A Winchester Road, Romsey ☎ 01794 513344.

Watchout!
- when joining the A3057 near Mottisfont.
- when crossing the busy A30.
- when cycling along Stockbridge High Street.

Link Information
This ride links with both the Stockbridge ride (route 26, point 1) and the Romsey ride (route 23, point 1) if you wish to explore the Test Valley further.

Refreshments

Horsebridge - John of Gaunt (friendly welcome and good value food) ☎ 01794 388394.

Mottisfont - Mottisfont Post Office Tearooms ☎ 01794 340243.

Broughton - Tally Ho! (excellent real ales) ☎ 01794 301280.

Longstock - Peat Spade (good quality food) ☎ 01264 810262.

Stockbridge - various pubs, tea room and café.

Picnic - Mottisfont Abbey Gardens and along the Test Way

A most enjoyable ride that delves into the delights of the Test Valley and its surrounding chalk downland. Excellent level cycling along the old 'Sprat and Winkle' railway line, close to the idyllic River Test, undulating quiet lanes and good downland tracks affording scenic views, combine to make this a splendid way to explore the Test Valley. Danebury Ring, Mottisfont Abbey and the attractive village of Stockbridge add to the charm of this ride.

START
Horsebridge. A tiny hamlet located off the A3057, 3 miles south of Stockbridge, just beyond Kings Somborne. Park in the Test Way car park opposite the John of Gaunt pub. OS grid ref: SU345304.

ROUTE DIRECTIONS
1. Take the path at the end of the car park and turn left along the Test Way, passing the old Horsebridge railway station. Head south through the Test Valley, on a level, good surfaced trackway for, 2miles (3.2km) eventually reaching a parking area and the A3057.

2. Turn right, then after 200 yards turn right again, signposted Mottisfont. Cross the River Test and shortly pass the visitors entrance to Mottisfont Abbey (NT) on the right. Continue through the village, bearing right by the tearoom, (turn left to join the Romsey ride) and remain on this gently undulating lane for 2½ miles (4km), with beautiful Test Valley views.

3. Take the first lane left, signposted Broughton. Head uphill, keeping right at the next junction, to follow the scenic lane through the valley of the Wallop Brook. Proceed into Broughton village centre to the Tally Ho! pub if in need of refreshment, otherwise, turn right on the edge of the village and cross a footbridge beside a ford in the river.

4. Keep straight on, the metalled lane soon petering out to a wide grass centred track that gradually climbs out of the valley. Proceed ahead at a junction of tracks and reach a lane after ¾ mile (1.2km). Bear right along the lane to reach the A30 Stockbridge to Salisbury road.

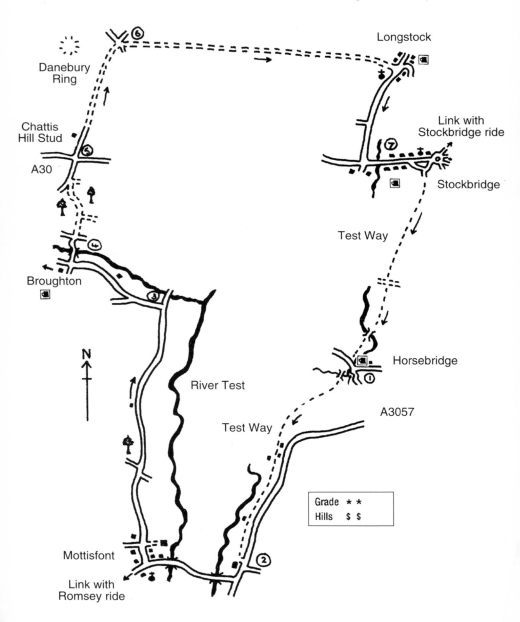

Longstock

Danebury Ring

Chattis Hill Stud

A30

Link with Stockbridge ride

Stockbridge

Test Way

Broughton

Test Way

River Test

N

Horsebridge

A3057

Test Way

Mottisfont

Link with Romsey ride

Grade ★ ★
Hills $ $

6. Cross over (care to be taken) into Spitfire Lane and pass Chattis Hill Stud. In ½ mile (0.8km), where the tarmac ends, bear slightly left along a wide trackway that drops downhill then climbs steadily to a junction of lanes. To visit the tree encircled mound of Danebury Ring, turn left, then first right.

The beautiful garden at Mottisfont Abbey.

7. The main route bears right, then immediately left onto an established arrowed by-way. Soon, descend into the Test Valley to the attractive village of Longstock. At a T-junction with the village lane, turn right (Peat Spade Inn a few yards left) and follow this valley lane for 1½ miles (2.4km) to the A30 and turn left into Stockbridge.

8. Proceed along the length of the High Street and turn right before the large roundabout, passing the Gamekeepers Restaurant. (Proceed ahead to the roundabout to link with the beginning of the Stockbridge ride). Turn left into Trafalgar Way and soon bear right to rejoin the Test Way. Remain on this excellent track, crossing the Clarendon Way, to the lane at Horsebridge. Turn left back to the car park.

ROUTE 16

BOURNE VALLEY AND THE CHUTES FROM HURSTBOURNE TARRANT

22 miles (35.3km) / 2 miles (3.2km) off-road.

OS Map
Landranger 185 (Winchester and Basingstoke) 1:50,000.

Nearest Railway Station
Andover, 7½ miles (12km) north.

Cycle Shops
1 Track Cycles, Love Lane, Andover
☎ 01264 332986.
Andover Bicycle Centre Union Street,
☎ 01264 352046.

Watchout!
- when crossing all main roads
- when descending off Conholt Hill towards Upton

Link Information
To explore the rolling hills and combes of North Hampshire further this route can be extended to include the short and undulating Walbury Hill ride (route 27 point 4).

Refreshments:

Stoke - White Hart Inn (locals' pub) ☎ 01264 738355.

Smannell - British Oak (traditional locals' pub/no food Sunday lunchtime) ☎ 01264 352964.

Tangley - Fox Inn (just off route/isolated/good hearty food, ales and wines) ☎ 01264 70276. Cricketers ☎ 01264 70283.

Lower Chute - Hatchett (charming thatched pub/good food and ale) ☎ 01264 730229.

Upton - Crown (no children) ☎ 01264 76265.

Hurstbourne Tarrant - George and Dragon (old coaching inn) ☎ 01264 76277.

A delightful ride mainly along quiet country lanes and two good sections of track, linking some of North Hampshire's charming villages. An undulating route that explores the Bourne Valley and gradually climbs to the top of Conholt Hill and the Chute Causeway, affording splendid views. Plenty of watering-holes to choose from along the way to quench thirst and restore energy.

START
Hurstbourne Tarrant. Parking area beside the A343 Andover to Newbury road, 2 miles (3.2km) north east of the village, beyond the entrance to Essebourne Manor Hotel. OS grid ref: SU406550.

The village green at Lower Chute.

ROUTE DIRECTIONS
1. From the car park follow the lane left off the A343 and in a mile (1.6km) climb steadily to reach a T-junction. Turn right steeply downhill into Stoke, passing the White Hart to reach a T-junction with the B3048. Bear left, then almost immediately turn right, signposted

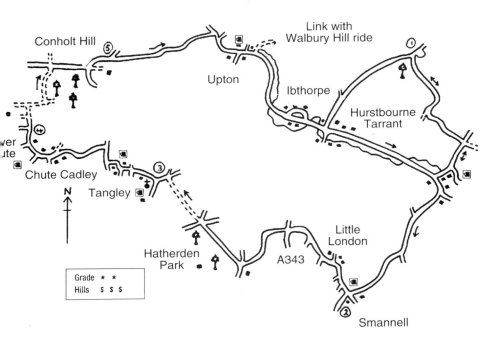

Smannell and ascend steeply out of the Bourne Valley. The lane soon levels out, affording open views south across Andover and generally descends for 1½ miles (2.4km) into Smannell.

2. At the junction beside the British Oak pub, turn right towards Little London and in ½ mile (0.8km) bear sharp left uphill by the access road to the village. Proceed for a mile (1.6km) to reach the A343. Cross straight over, signed Penton Mewsey, then after ¾ mile (1.2km) take the second lane right (unsigned), just before the Hare and Hounds pub. Follow this narrow lane beside Hatherden Park to a junction of five-ways and cross over onto the only unmetalled route, climbing uphill on a wide stony track. Gradually ascend on this old Roman Road for a mile (1.6km) to reach a lane.

3. Turn left beside cottages and keep left at a fork if requiring refreshment at the Fox Inn. Otherwise, bear right to pass Tangley church, then dip and rise to a

ALONG THE WAY

Tangley
A scattered village spread along numerous tree-lined lanes that criss-cross this well-wooded and hilly parish. The off-road section between Hatherden and Tangley follows the old Roman Road that once linked Winchester to Cirencester, which at the time was one of the largest towns in the country. Tangley church - St Thomas - enjoys a peaceful spot beside Fox plantation. It boasts the only lead font in Hampshire and one of only thirty similar fonts that survive in England. It dates from the 17th-century and is decorated with thistles and roses.

The Chutes
Attractive collection of five hamlets - Upper, Lower, Chute Standen, Chute Forest and Chute Cadley - nestling in hilly and little visited border country between Wiltshire and Hampshire. The highest point of the ride follows Chute Causeway, originally part of the Roman Highway from Winchester to Mildenhall. It affords fine views south across Hampshire.

Hurstbourne Tarrant
Set beside one of Hampshire's most charming and unspoilt river valleys, the Bourne Valley, this picturesque village originated as a Saxon settlement known as 'Hisseburnas'. The addition of Tarrant to the village name is attributed to the former owner of the manor, a community of Cistercian nuns at Tarrant Crawford in Dorset. During the early 19th-century, a regular visitor was William Cobbett of 'Rural Rides' fame, who referred to the village as Uphusband, 'husband' being a dialect form of Hurstbourne. The church houses some rare 14th-century wall paintings and the George and Dragon, a 16th-century coaching inn, displays the original mail-rack where letters delivered by coach awaited collection. Neighbouring Ibthorpe, a peaceful hamlet beside the River Swift, consists of a collection of thatched and timbered houses and some fine Georgian farmhouses. Jane Austen was a frequent visitor to Ibthorpe House, once the home of her friend Mary Lloyd.

crossroads by a memorial cross. Proceed across into the main village of Tangley, bearing right, then left by the Cricketers pub, soon to reach a T-junction. Turn right, signed Conholt, then after 200 yards take the narrow lane left for The Chutes. Shortly, freewheel down into Chute Cadley, keeping right by the green in Lower Chute to pass the charming thatched pub - The Hatchet.

4. Continue along this lane, signed Upper Chute and in ½ mile (0.8km) enter Chute Standen. Where the lane bears sharp left at a grass triangle, keep straight on a 'No Through Road' and soon pass the entrance to Standen House. The tarmac gives way to a good bridleway beside its grounds, then at a T-junction of tracks turn right and shortly follow it left, ascending steadily uphill to reach a lane on top of Little Down. Turn right along Chute Causeway, a fine lane beside Conholt Park that affords splendid views south into Hampshire.

5. At a T-junction, opposite the entrance to Conholt House, turn left, signed Vernham Dean. In ¼ mile (0.4km) at the top of Conholt Hill, bear off right onto a narrow single track road towards Upton. With fine views north across the rolling landscape of the North Hampshire Hills, soon descend quickly to a T-junction. Turn right and follow the valley bottom road through Upton, (link with Walbury Hill ride here), then beside the intermittently flowing River Swift to reach Ibthorpe and the A343 in Hurstbourne Tarrant. Turn right, then almost immediately left beside the George and Dragon onto the B3048, signed Stoke. Proceed through the village, then follow the infant Bourne River for 1½ miles (2.4km) into Stoke, turning left, signed Binley, and retrace your outward route back to the car park.

NORTH HAMPSHIRE BORDER LANES AND DOWNLAND AROUND KINGSCLERE

15½ miles (24.7km) / 1¾ miles (2.8km) off-road

OS Maps
Landranger 174 (Newbury and Wantage) and 185 (Winchester and Basingstoke) 150,000.

Nearest Railway Station
Overton, 5 miles (8km) south.

Cycle Shops/Hire
Raleigh Cycle Centre (spares/repairs), 22 Winchester Street, Basingstoke
☎ 01256 465266.
Winklebury Cycles, (spares/hire) Winklebury Centre, Basingstoke, 3 miles (4.8km from point 4)
☎ 01256 20645 & 331444.
Mountain Movers (spares/hire), Weighmore House, Crockford Lane, Chineham, Basingstoke
☎ 01256 8141438.

Watchout! -
- when crossing the A339 twice.
- on the blind bends on the narrow lanes.
- on the steep and bumpy track off Plantation Hill.

Link Information
By turning left at the crossroads in Ramsdell you can link with the Silchester ride (route 25, point 3) to explore the North Hampshire lanes and Calleva Roman Town further. This in turn links with the Wellington Country Park ride (route 28, point 2).

A fairly short and not-too-energetic cycle ride around the web of tiny lanes that exist on the Hampshire/Berkshire border, between Kingsclere and Tadley. The route becomes hillier in the latter section, as it climbs onto downland towards Hannington, returning to Kingsclere via good tracks.

START
Kingsclere. Large village set just off the A339 between Basingstoke and Newbury, 7 miles north west of Basingstoke. Park in the free car park located behind the newsagents along Swan Street in the village centre, opposite the church. OS grid ref SU525586.

ROUTE DIRECTIONS
1. Leave the car park and return to the main village road beside the newsagents and opposite the church. Turn right along Swan Street, then at the T-junction opposite the Crown, turn left and follow this road through the village to a roundabout on the A339 Newbury to Basingstoke road. Take the second exit, Union Lane, and pass Kingsclere Park (Industrial Estate). Continue on this level, narrow and twisty lane for 2½ miles (4km) through Plaistow Green to reach a T-junction.

2. Turn right, then after ½ mile (0.8km) enter Ashford Hill and descend to the B3051. Turn right, signed Kingsclere and soon pass Hussey's Bakery on your right. Take the next lane left for Wheat Hold and Wolverton Common, a peaceful gently undulating lane. At a T-junction turn left, arrowed Axmansford, then bear almost immediately right onto an unsigned narrow lane. Meander past Ham Farmhouse to a T-junction on the edge of Baughurst.

3. Turn right and then left after 100 yards towards Ramsdell and enter Stony Heath. Keep right at the next junction, following this level road for a further 1¾

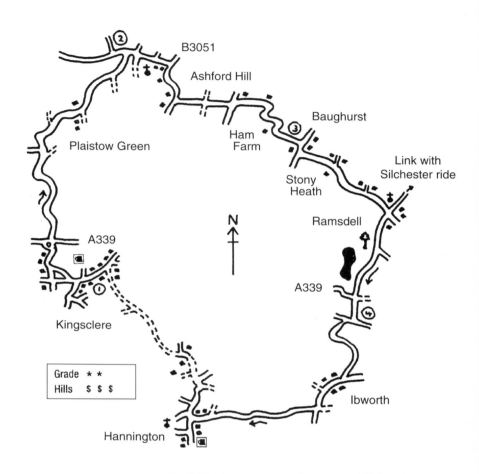

miles(2.8km) to a crossroads in Ramsdell, beside the tiny church. (Turn left at the crossroads to link with the Silchester ride). Turn right, signposted Ewhurst onto a narrow lane that gently descends past Ewhurst Park to reach the A339.

4. Taking great care at this fast and busy road, turn right and almost immediately left onto a tiny lane, signed Ibworth. Now begin the steady climb onto rolling downland to the attractive hamlet of Ibworth. At a T-junction, turn right through the cluster of houses, then bear off right at a junction on a bend, towards Hannington. Descend rapidly and climb steadily on a quiet lane into the high downland village of Hannington.

Refreshments

Kingsclere - Crown, Market Place ☎ 01635 298311. Swan, Swan Street ☎ 01635 298314. George and Horn, George Street ☎ 01635 298281. Off Licence Café, Swan Street.

Hannington - Vine (good range of real ales and fine summer garden) ☎ 01635 298525.

The downland church of All Saints at Hannington.

ALONG THE WAY

Kingsclere
A substantial village - once a royal hunting estate, as its name suggests - situated at the base of rolling downland and noted race-horse training gallops. The settlement developed at a meeting of several important roads, and had fairs and markets in medieval times and a great diversity of employment, including four mills. Today, it is a dormitory settlement for nearby Basingstoke and Newbury.

Hannington
Situated high up on the downs, this attractive village surrounds a small green which has an unusual roofed well. The ancient church of All Saints is a mixture of styles and boasts two modern engraved windows, both designed and engraved by Laurence Whistler.

At a T-junction, opposite the green and church turn left if wishing to visit the Vine pub. Otherwise, proceed right through the village.

5. Keep right, following the lane quickly downhill, then on reaching a barn on your right, turn left at the crossing of tracks and steeply ascend a good chalk track onto Plantation Hill. Bear right at a junction of tracks and soon bear left onto a metalled lane beyond a farmyard. Follow the lane left, then where it veers right, continue ahead on a wide bridleway and descend steeply off the down. The track can be wet and clayey, but affords good rural views. Proceed for ½ mile (0.8km), keep right at a fork of routes and soon descend into Kingsclere. On merging with tarmac, keep right to reach a road, opposite the George and Horn pub. Bear left, then left again into the village centre and shortly return via Swan Street to the car park.

OX-DROVES, TRACKS AND QUIET LANES AROUND MEDSTEAD

13 miles (20.8km) / 5 miles (8km) off-road

OS Map
Landranger 185 (Winchester and Basingstoke) 1:50,000.

Nearest Railway Station
Alton, 5 miles (8km) east.

Cycle Shops
Watts Cycles, 3 Station Road, Alresford
☎ 01962 733145.
Ransomes Cycle, Victoria Road, Alton
☎ 01420 82867.
Hampshire Cycle Centre, High Street,
Alton ☎ 01420 82562.

Link Information
For an extended tour along the byways and lanes that abound in this beautiful area, it is worth linking up with the Preston Candover ride (route 21, point 4), 1½ miles (2.4km) from Bradley. It is also possible to link this ride with the Alresford ride (route 8, point 3) by diverting ¾ mile (1.2km) from Lower Wield.

Refreshments

Lower Wield - Yew Tree (good food/garden) ☎ 01256 389224.

Bentworth - Star Inn
☎ 01420 561005, Sun (good pub food/range of real ales)
☎ 01420 562338.

ALONG THE WAY

Four Marks
Of particular interest is the Watercress Line, Hampshire's rural steam railway which runs through ten miles of rolling countryside between Alresford

A combination of old ox-droves and narrow traffic-free lanes make this short and undulating ride most enjoyable. A few charming small hamlets, unspoilt country views and two notable pubs for refreshment. Some of the off-road sections may be wet and muddy in winter.

START

Medstead. Free parking area at Chawton Park Wood, located ½ mile (0.8km) north of the A31 Winchester to Farnham road at Four Marks. OS grid ref: SU672361.

ROUTE DIRECTIONS

1. Leave the car park by the rear exit and proceed along the single track on the left until it joins the main track through Chawton Park Wood. Turn right down the track to a T-junction at the bottom, turn left, then after 100 yards take the right-hand fork and continue to the crossing of three routes. Turn right along the bridleway and head uphill to the edge of the wood and continue to a road beside farm buildings. Cross straight over and follow a track to the main Medstead to Bentworth lane (by a postbox).

2. Again cross over onto a further track, then in ½ mile (0.8km) at a waymarked junction turn left uphill, soon to disregard the bridleway on your left in 100 yards. On reaching a T-junction, turn left, then first right, signed Lower Wield. Pass the Yew Tree pub, then turn right, arrowed Bradley. (Proceed ahead for 1½ miles (2.4km) to link with Alresford ride.) Cycle through the hamlet of Lower Wield, keeping ahead for Bradley. Gradually descend into Bradley, pass the telephone box and the village pond and take the next track on your right. Keep to the lane to a staggered crossroads and turn left for 1½ miles (2.4km) to reach Preston Candover and the beginning of Route 21.

3. In 100 yards cross a further track and remain on the track for a mile (1.6km) to reach a lane. Turn right, then almost immediately right again, signposted Burkham and Bentworth. Follow this narrow lane for 2 miles (3.2km) to a crossroads and proceed straight across into Bentworth. Pass the school and church, then at the Star Inn turn left. In ¼ mile (0.4km) turn right, signed Shaldon and descend past the Sun pub, an excellent place for refreshment.

4. Shortly, as the road bears left, take the right fork downhill and soon climb uphill to pass Childer Hill Farm on your right. Continue pedalling uphill, then at the top, beyond Heathcroft Farm, turn right onto a bridleway. At the end of the track near Theddon Grange, continue onto the road, turning right past the farm buildings, soon to pass through the hamlet of Wivelrod. At a T-junction turn right into Abbey Road, signed Medstead. After 100 yards turn left onto a bridleway, just beyond the Medstead village sign. From here retrace your outward route back to Chawton Wood car park.

and Alton and stopping at Ropley & Four Marks. There are various events and steam days. ☎ 01962 733810.

Bentworth
Situated among the closely folded hills on the south eastern end of the Hampshire Downs, Bentworth is an attractive village comprising some fine large houses, thatched cottages and farms. St Mary's church is mainly 13th-century with the Early English style dominating the interesting interior. Lookout for the medieval font, complete with pyrimidal wooden cover dated 1605. The churchyard is home to a flourishing thorn that was grafted from the Holy Thorn planted by Joseph of Arimathea at Glastonbury.

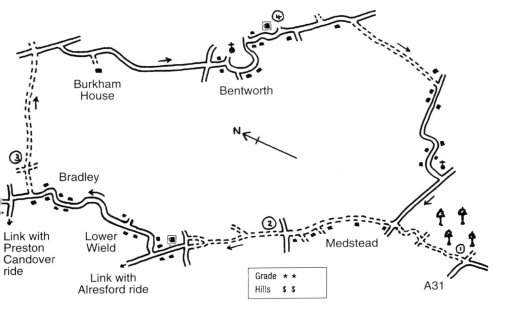

DOWNLAND TRACKS AND THE DEVER VALLEY FROM MICHELDEVER WOOD

24½ miles (39km) / 8½ miles (13.5km) off-road

OS Map
Landranger 185 (Winchester and Basingstoke) 1:50,000.

Nearest Railway Station
Micheldever Station, 2½ miles (4km) north of Micheldever and point 7 of the ride.

Cycle Shops/Hire
Peter Hansford Cycles (repairs/hire), 91 Olivers Battery Road South, Winchester ☎ 01962 877555.
Mike's Bikes (hire) ☎ 01962 885651.
Peter Hargroves Cycles, 26 Jewry Street, Winchester ☎ 01962 860005.
1 Track Cycles, Love Lane, Andover ☎ 01264 332986.
Andover Bicycle Centre, Union Street, Andover ☎ 01264 352046.

Watchout!
- when crossing the A33 (twice) and A30 trunk roads.
- stretches of off-road biking can be boggy in winter.

Link Information
For a tough day's ride this route links with the Stockbridge ride (route 26, point 2). On reaching the T-junction on the edge of Chilbolton (point 4), bear left through the village to reach the A3057 at West Down car park by the River Test and turn right over the bridge, passing the Mayfly pub.

A lengthy, yet not-too-demanding, ride through the heart of the county, exploring scenic downland tracks and bridleways between the Itchen and Test Valleys. The gently undulating return route follows delightfully peaceful lanes through the attractive hamlets and villages that nestle in the Dever Valley. Expect some of the bridleways to be wet and muddy in winter. It is advisable to allow plenty of time to complete the circuit.

START

Micheldever Wood. Situated 1 mile (1.6km) off the A33 Winchester to Basingstoke road at the Lunways Inn, 4½ miles (7.2km) north of Winchester. Car park and picnic area on the edge of the wood and archaeological trail. OS grid ref: SU530363.

ROUTE DIRECTIONS

1. From the woodland parking area, turn right along the lane, passing beneath the M3, then on reaching the A33 beside the Lunways Inn cross over the dual carriageway onto an excellent wide gravel farm track - The Lunway. Keep to this scenic bridleway in a westerly direction for 1½ miles (2.4km) to a crossroads by a thatched cottage.

2. Head straight across onto an arrowed 'Right of Way' - Wonston and Crawley, and follow a metalled farm road for ½ mile (0.8km) to a crossing of paths at the end of the tarmac. Keep ahead along a bridleway (can be muddy) and soon pass South Wonston farm. Again, continue straight on at a crossing of bridleways, and follow the access track out to a road. Turn left, then after 150 yards, turn right and pass beneath the A34.

3. Keep right onto a pitted tarmac track, parallel with A34 and soon bear left along a bumpy track. Gently descend to an unmarked crossing of tracks (numerous gates) and turn left onto a good track (keep dogs on leads sign), along the left-hand edge of an open field. On

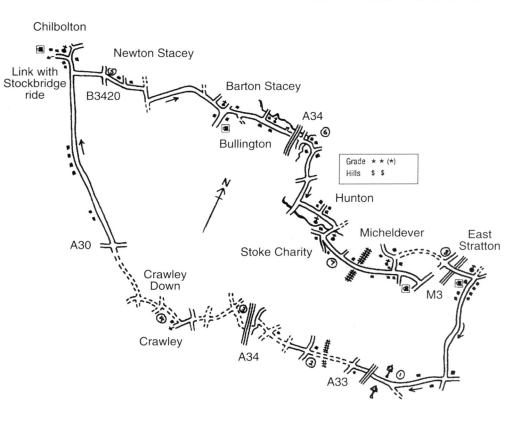

reaching a clump of coniferous trees and a fork of tracks, bear off diagonally right on a bridleway between fields and soon reach a lane junction. Go straight across, signposted Crawley, then in 200 yards, turn right onto a concrete track beneath a barrier.

4. Continue along a good grass-centred track across Crawley Down, keeping ahead at a crossing of paths to follow a bridleway through trees. Bear left, then after 100 yards turn right at a staggered crossing of tracks and leave the woodland. Proceed for ¾ mile (1.2km) to the A30. Taking great care, cross over towards Chilbolton and follow an undulating lane for 2 miles (3.2km) to a T-junction. (Turn left if seeking refreshment at the Abbot's Mitre in Chilbolton, or wishing to link with the Stockbridge ride). Otherwise, turn right to reach a crossroads at the B3420.

Refreshments

Chilbolton - Abbot's Mitre (pub)
☎ 01264 860348.

Barton Stacey - Swan Inn
☎ 01962 760470.

Micheldever - Dever Arms (good pub food) ☎ 01962 774339.

East Stratton - Plough Inn (simple country pub, hearty food)
☎ 0196289 241.

ALONG THE WAY

Micheldever Wood
This ancient woodland is believed to have been established in Saxon times and preserves a unique archaeological landscape which dates back into prehistory. A fascinating trail through the wood explores Bronze-Age burial monuments, an Iron Age settlement and Roman fields.

The Lunway
One of the many ancient cross-country routes that traversed the county. Once used as a droving route for sheep, this particular track linked Old Sarum in Wiltshire to Stockbridge, before progressing north of Winchester to join the Harrow Way near Basingstoke.

Micheldever
An extremely picturesque village, full of timber-framed cottages, many of which are thatched. The church of St Mary is very unusual, in fact quite odd from the outside. The original early 16th-century tower adjoins a brick octagonal nave.

5. Go across, signposted Newton Stacey, to join a quiet, narrow lane through the hamlet, then ascend steadily with fine views across the Test Valley, and soon drop downhill into Barton Stacey. At a T-junction, turn left (Swan Inn to right), then almost immediately right, opposite the church, arrowed Bullington. Climb out of the village, then head downhill into the Dever Valley. Pass Bullington church and proceed beneath the A34 to a T-junction.

6. Turn right, then left signed Norton and cross the River Dever. Follow the lane through the hamlet, ascending to a crossroads. Continue ahead signed Wonston and proceed downhill, turning left at the bottom, just before the river, arrowed Hunton. This delightful lane runs parallel to the River Dever and through the hamlet of Hunton, passing its tiny church on the right. Continue into Stoke Charity and turn left for Micheldever.

7. Keep to this rolling lane into Micheldever, turning left at the junction in the village centre. (Bear right, then first right for the Dever Arms). Pass the church and school, then turn right into Rook Lane. Where it bears left into Northbrook Avenue, keep ahead onto a bridleway and pass the sewage works. At a fork of paths, proceed straight on, uphill on a wide bridleway, soon to follow a narrow muddy tree-lined path for ¼ mile (0.4km) to reach the fast and busy A30.

8. Cross over, taking great care, to join the road for East Stratton and go over the M3. In the village follow the lane sharp right and soon pass the Plough Inn. Continue for 1½ miles (2.4km) to a crossroads near Northington Down Farm. Turn right and follow this lane for just over a mile (1.6km) back to the car park in Micheldever Wood.

CANAL TOWPATH AND SCENIC DOWNLAND TRACKS FROM ODIHAM

22 miles (35.2km) / 13½ miles (21.6km)

OS Map
Landranger 186 (Aldershot and Guildford) 1:50,000.

Nearest Railway Station
Hook, 3 miles (4.8km) north

Cycle Shops/Hire
Mountain Movers (hire), Weighmore House, Crockford Lane, Chineham, Basingstoke ☎ 01256 814138. Winklebury Cycles (hire), Winklebury Centre, Basingstoke ☎ 01256 20645 & 331444.

Watchout!
- along the towpath; it can be narrow and bumpy in places and is perilously close to the water at times.
- when crossing both the A32 and the busy A287.
- on the stony section of byway near Well and some of the other bumpy and awkward to ride bridleways.

Refreshments

Odiham - various pubs and tea rooms.

Winchfield Hurst - Old Barley Mow Tea Rooms (beside canal). Barley Mow ☎ 01252 617490.

Well - Chequers (character pub/good garden, ale and food) ☎ 01256 862605.

Upton Grey - Hoddington Arms (decent pub food and good garden) ☎ 01256 862371.

Greywell - Fox and Goose ☎ 01256 702062

A most varied and enjoyable ride through this attractive corner of Hampshire, incorporating the peaceful towpath beside the well restored Basingstoke Canal, little used lanes and undulating off-road tracks, some of which can be demanding, especially after wet weather. Delightful views and charming villages result in an interesting route through unspoilt countryside.

START

Odiham. A small country town located just off the B3349 between Reading and Alton and 2 miles (3.2km) from the M3 at junction 5. Park in Odiham Wharf car park at Colt Hill, situated to the north of the High Street (canal signposted). OS grid ref: SU747517.

ROUTE DIRECTIONS

1. From the car park turn left along the canal towpath and keep to this peaceful stretch of restored canal for 3½ miles (5.6km) to reach a bridge beyond Tundry Pond (information board on war defences). Continue to the next bridge, pass beneath and bear sharp left up onto the road. Turn left across the canal and follow this gently undulating lane for a mile (1.6km) to a T-junction with the A287 Farnham to Basingstoke road. Turn left, then almost immediately bear right (great care) onto a narrow lane, signposted Hillside and Roke.

2. In 100 yards bear left at a T-junction (unsigned), then shortly veer right beside a house to join a wide trackway that steadily climbs uphill, passing Calf Lane Quarry. At a barn, follow the hedged track left and begin to descend to a lane. Keep left uphill and in ¾ mile (1.2km) turn right at a T-junction, signed Countryscene. Pass Penn Croft Farm, then as the lane curves left, keep ahead along a narrow metalled lane through open farmland and continue to Swanthorpe Farm and Stables. Here the tarmac gives way to a very stony and awkward to ride on track (can be wet in winter). The surface soon improves

ALONG THE WAY

Odiham

Charming small town that remains relatively unspoilt, retaining its medieval street plan and country atmosphere, despite being close to the fast-expanding settlements of Basingstoke, Fleet and Aldershot. Delightful winding main street lined with mainly Georgian houses with mellow-brick frontages and upmarket specialist shops. Also of interest are the Tudor vicarage and the fine 14th-century church, supposedly the largest church in North Hampshire. Note the unusual 'Pest House' in the churchyard which used to house the unfortunate victims of the Plague in 1665.

and gently ascend to reach a lane in ½ mile (0.8km).

3. Bear right and enter the village of Well, keeping left at a junction by the village pond, (Chequers pub a short distance right), and climb to a crossroads by an old covered well. Go straight across, signed Froyle, onto a single-track road and soon take the arrowed right of way on your right. Initially very stony and often rutted, keep to this scenic undulating byway as it ascends through the edge of woodland, soon to reach a lane and crossroads at Sutton Common. Turn left uphill, then at a T-junction (unsigned) turn right and gradually climb on quiet lane, affording fine rural views north, to reach an unsigned crossroads at the edge of woodland.

4. Turn right and descend on a narrow metalled track to a T-junction and bear right, continuing downhill for ½ mile (0.8km), soon to take the waymarked 'Right of Way

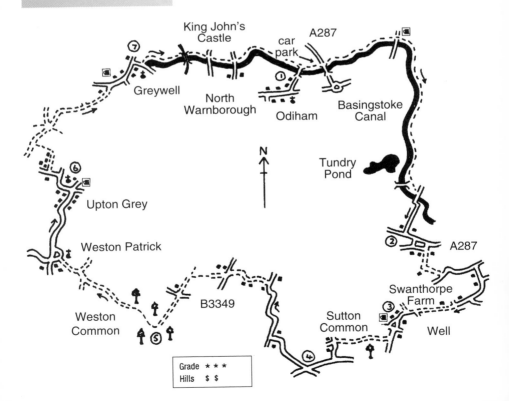

Grade ★ ★ ★
Hills $ $

on your left. Descend the rough track, passing two dwellings to reach the often busy B3349. Bear left, diagonally crossing the road (great care) to join an arrowed Right of Way, beside the driveway to Old Meadows. Climb a narrow hedged path, soon to bear left at a junction of routes and descend on a good wide bridleway to a metalled track. Cross straight over to follow a tarmac drive that gently descends to a gate beside a house on a woodland fringe (Weston Common).

5. Beyond the gate turn immediately right along the hedge to follow a bridleway (can be very muddy after rain) through the edge of the wood. Leave the wood behind and keep to a grass-centred track along the right-hand edge of a large field. Remain on this quite bumpy well defined track (tricky and tiring) for a mile (1.6km) to reach a farm track. Bear right, then in a few yards where the track curves right, proceed ahead and descend to a gate and lane in the village of Weston Patrick. Turn left, then at a crossroads turn right to follow the valley bottom road for a mile (1.6km) into the attractive village of Upton Grey.

6. At the village pond, turn left signed Tunworth and climb through the village, passing the church and the lane for Greywell, and soon turn right along Cleves Lane. Where the lane forks, bear left onto the wide gravel track and follow this through open farmland with views towards Basingstoke to a T-junction of tracks. Turn right and gently ascend on a chalky track to a junction of five routes at a clump of beech trees (Five Lanes End). Bear slightly right and keep ahead, soon to descend a good bridleway, eventually passing farm buildings to reach a lane. Turn right and enter the charming village of Greywell.

7. Just beyond the Fox and Goose turn right into Deptford Lane and almost immediately take the arrowed footpath left - Basingstoke Canal and Greywell Tunnel. Negotiate a tight squeeze stile and walk your bike for a short distance to reach the canal towpath. Keep to the towpath, passing King John's Castle, for 2 miles (3.2km) back into Odiham and the Wharfside car park.

Basingstoke Canal
Completed in 1794 to transport timber, grain and malt from North Hampshire to London, returning with coal and various manufactured goods, this once popular commercial route climbed 37 miles through Surrey via a total of 29 locks. The waterway also had 69 bridges, two aqueducts, a variety of active wharfs and warehouses and the longest canal tunnel in Southern England. The coming of the railways led to the gradual decline of the canal, although it was used to transport materials for the construction of Aldershot Barracks in the 1850's and for shifting munitions during the First World War. After 25 years of gradual restoration 32 miles of the canal were reopened in 1991 as a leisure amenity.

King John's Castle (AM)
Also referred to as Odiham Castle, the surviving ruins of this historic building enjoy a peaceful position overlooking the Basingstoke Canal. Built in 1212, it is noted as the place from where King John set out from to sign the Magna Carta.

Greywell
Consisting of predominantly 17th-century brick and timber cottages, this delightful village is set beside the River Whitewater. The medieval St Mary's church boasts a fine 16th-century rood screen and an unusual stair-turret giving access to the rood. Greywell Tunnel was built in 1792 and at 1,230 yards was the longest canal tunnel in southern England. Since its collapse in 1934, it has become one of the most important bat roosts in Britain.

SCENIC BYWAYS, BRIDLEWAYS AND LANES FROM PRESTON CANDOVER

12 miles (19.3km) / 7 miles (11.2km) off-road

OS Map
Landranger 185 (Winchester and Basingstoke) 1:50,000.

Nearest Railway Station
Basingstoke or Micheldever.

Cycle Shops/Hire
Mountain Movers (hire), Weighmore House, Crockford Lane, Chineham, Basingstoke ☎ 01256 814138. Winklebury Cycles (hire), Winklebury Centre, Basingstoke ☎ 01256 20645 & 331444. Raleigh Cycle Centre, 22 Winchester Street, Basingstoke ☎ 01256 465266.

Watchout!
- some of the byways are severely rutted by 4-wheel drive activity.

Link Information
Two short diversions can be made to link with the Medstead ride (route 18, point 2) and to extend your ride from Preston Candover to explore the Alresford ride (route 8, point 3).

A short undulating ride across attractive downland, using some of the excellent tracks that criss-cross the unspoilt farmland and woodland in the area. Delightful rolling downland views and Dummer village and church are worth exploring. A few of the tracks can be rutted and muddy during the winter months.

START

Preston Candover. Small village located on the B3046 between Basingstoke and Alresford, 7 miles (11.2km) south of Basingstoke. Parking area situated opposite the school on the B-road. OS grid ref: SU607417.

ROUTE DIRECTIONS

1. From the parking area turn right along the B3046, passing the lane for Wield (follow this if wishing to extend ride, by linking with Alresford route in a mile (1.6km)), and the church, then bear off right along a T-road on the edge of the village. Keep left, the metalled surface soon giving way to a stony track that climbs steadily out of the valley. The gradient eases as the track crosses open farmland with good all-round views. At a junction, follow the waymarked byway left, then in 200 yards turn right off the gravel track onto the rutted byway (arrowed) beside trees.

2. Continue for ¾ mile (1.2km) to reach a lane. Turn left, then in about ½ mile (0.8km) take the signed Right of Way on your right along the metalled driveway to Dummer Grange (Wayfarers Walk). Keep left by the entrance to the house, uphill and right on a gravel track. Soon bear left by a cottage and keep to this good track for ¾ mile (1.2km) into the village of Dummer. Turn right at a lane and immediately keep right by the church, signed Farleigh Wallop. Follow the lane left for the Queen pub.

3. Gently ascend on this narrow lane, affording fine open views, for nearly 2 miles (3.2km) to reach the B3046. Turn left, signposted Basingstoke, and shortly turn right at a crossroads towards Farleigh House. Cycle through the hamlet of Farleigh Wallop, then just before a sharp downhill stretch, bear off right to join an arrowed bridleway and freewheel down a pitted track towards a thatched cottage. Go through a gate and keep to a good gravel track through the valley (Bedlam Bottom) to a further gate. Continue through peaceful woodland, eventually reaching a lane beside a large thatched house.

Refreshments

Preston Candover - Purefoy Arms
☎ 01256 389258.

Dummer - Queen (popular food pub) ☎ 01256 397367.

Ellisfield - Fox (range of real ales/food/garden)
☎ 01256 383210.

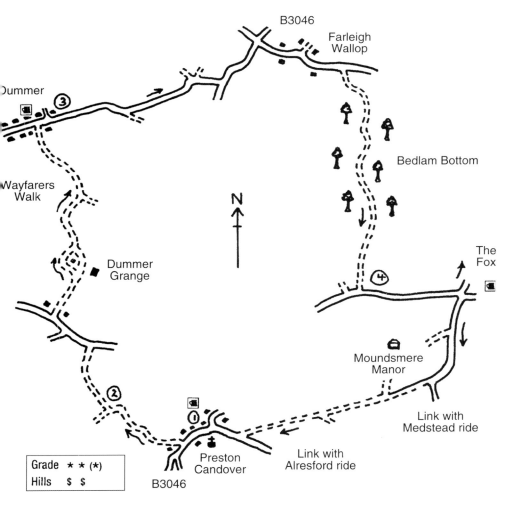

Grade ★ ★ (★)
Hills $ $

ALONG THE WAY

Preston Candover
One of three Candover villages nestling in this charming valley, the word Candover originating from the word 'Dever' which means water crossing.

Wayfarers Walk
A long-distance walking trail that traverses Hampshire, extending 70 miles between Emsworth on the south coast to Inkpen Beacon just across the Berkshire border.

Dummer
An attractive downland village divided into Up Street and Down Street and incorporating dwellings from several periods, including numerous picturesque thatched cottages. The treasure of the village is the 12th-century Church of All Saints which has numerous interesting features. It has a large panelled medieval roof canopy above the chancel arch, a rare surviving example and unique to Hampshire. The splendid pulpit dates from 1380 and is one of the six oldest in England. One notable preacher who spoke from this pulpit was George Whitefield who was a follower of Wesley. Located near the Queen pub is the old village well, which has a well preserved 10-foot-diameter wooden tread-wheel.

One of the many quiet tracks in the Candover Valley.

4. Turn left and cycle for a mile into Ellisfield, soon to turn right at a crossroads, signed Bradley (Turn left for a ½ mile (0.8km) ride to the Fox pub). Climb steadily through Preston Oak Hills Wood, pass the entrance to Moundsmere Manor, then on reaching a sharp right-hand bend, keep straight on along a waymarked byway. (Keep to the lane for ½ mile (0.8km) and go over a crossroads into Bradley to link with the Medstead ride). Remain on this tree-lined track (can be very wet and muddy in winter) for just over a mile (1.6km) to a lane. Follow it right to a T-junction on the edge of Preston Candover and turn left along the B3046 back to your car.

QUEEN ELIZABETH COUNTRY PARK AND THE SOUTH DOWNS WAY

11½ miles (18.5km) / 6½ miles (10.4km) off-road

OS Map
Landranger 197 (Chichester and The Downs) 1:50,000.

Nearest Railway Station
Petersfield, 4 miles (6.4km) north.

Cycle Hire
Available at the Gravel Hill car park in the Queen Elizabeth Country Park, located behind the Centre (for use in the Country Park only).
4 Bikes Warehouse Horndean, 3 miles (4.8km) south ☎ 01705 591018.

Watchout!
- woodland trails and the South Downs Way are popular with both horse-riders and ramblers.
- some tracks can be very muddy and slippery in winter.
- steep descents on the South Downs Way.

A fairly challenging ride on undulating lanes, downland tracks and woodland bridleways, incorporating the South Downs Way and venturing into West Sussex. Excellent off-road biking, although these sections can be demanding after prolonged rain. Beautiful scenery and views from the South Downs.

START

Queen Elizabeth Country Park. Signposted off the A3, 4 miles (6.4km) south of Petersfield. Pay and display car park in front of the Park Centre. OS grid ref: SU719185.

ROUTE DIRECTIONS

1. From the car park, follow the metalled lane to the right of the Park Centre into the Country Park, (signed mountain bike route). Where the road veers left to a further parking area, bear off right onto a track into a 'no public access' area and follow the blue arrow left. Just before a works yard, bear right onto a good bridleway and follow this parallel to the A3 and around the fringe of Queen Elizabeth Forest. Dip and climb, eventually leaving the woodland behind to follow the rolling fenced trackway to a lane.

Refreshments

Queen Elizabeth Country Park - Park Centre Café

Chalton - Red Lion
☎ 01705 592246.

Picnic - in the Country Park and along the South Downs Way.

2. Turn right for 100 yards to reach the entrance to Buster Ancient Farm, otherwise turn left uphill and soon enter the village of Chalton.(Turn right to visit Buster Ancient Farm, entrance 200 yards.) At the next junction, turn left signposted Ditcham and Idmiston, (keep straight on to visit Chalton church and for refreshment at the Red Lion), and climb uphill. Descend rapidly passing a lane on the left and soon cross a bridge over the railway. Proceed down the valley, soon to turn left at the next junction (not waymarked) and gently ascend with the isolated Idmiston Church in the field to your right.

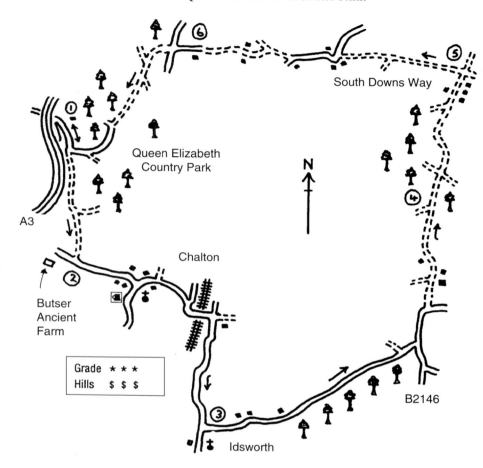

3. Continue on this delightful narrow lane, gradually
ascending below Compton Down, then freewheel downhill
to the B2146. Turn left, then in 200 yards, bear off left onto
a waymarked bridleway towards Hucksholt Farm. Keep
ahead at a junction of tracks and fingerpost and soon pass
through double gates onto a grass-centred track. Gradually
ascend towards woodland.

4. Proceed straight on at the next junction of
bridleways and shortly cross a forest track, to follow a
good track beyond a gate along the fringe of
woodland. Remain on this bridleway, soon to pass
Foxcombe House and ascend on a metalled access road
past cottages to a crossing of tracks beyond a house

called 'Downlands'. Turn left onto the South Downs Way.

5. Gently undulate, views opening up across Petersfield to your right, then descend steeply to a lane and Sunwood Farm. Turn left and follow the lane uphill for ¼ mile (0.4km) towards an isolated house. Just before reaching the house, bear off right onto a metalled farm track and head gently downhill, passing an old 'Cart Track for Buriton', and a building hidden in trees. Ascend steeply on the South Downs Way and soon drop downhill to merge with a tarmac track near some cottages.

6. At a crossroads, go straight across into the Forestry Commission parking area. Pass through a small waymarked gate and climb steeply on a good track, back into the Queen Elizabeth Country Park. Remain on this defined track, disregarding routes left and right and descend through the forest to reach a metalled forest track, beyond a kiosk and seating area. Bear left and soon rejoin the outward route back to the Park Centre and car park.

Buster Ancient Farm
Fascinating re-creation of an Iron Age farmhouse and fields. The earthworks, the roundhouses, the fences and fields, the crops and livestock are all part of an open-air research project, which since 1972, has been working towards a greater understanding of prehistoric buildings and agriculture. Open daily March to November (winter by arrangement).
☎ 01705 598838

Chalton
A small village nestling amid the downs beneath a hill crowned by Chalton windmill. The Red Lion is reputedly the oldest pub in Hampshire, dating from 1147 and its attractive black and white timbered exterior is topped with a heavy, overhanging thatched roof. Opposite the pub lies the 12th-century church of St Michael which has a notable decorated east window.

South Downs Way
This long-distance trail follows the length of the South Downs, a range of rounded, smooth chalk hills, from Eastbourne in Sussex to Winchester in the Hampshire basin; a total of 100 miles (160km). The hills are not high and the terrain is not strenuous, but the route provides variety in both scenery and physical demands.

Scenic bridleway between Queen Elizabeth Country Park and Butser Ancient Farm.

A RURAL RIDE AROUND ROMSEY

16½ miles (27km) all road

OS Map
Landranger 185 (Winchester and Basingstoke) 1:50,000.

Nearest Railway Station
Romsey.

Cycle Shops
Cycle World, 109 Winchester Road, Romsey ☎ 01794 513344. Abbey Cycles and Accessories, 70 Cherbille Street, Romsey ☎ 01794 515328.

Watchout!
- on the main A31 through and into Romsey. Some of the lanes are very narrow with blind corners.

Link Information
This route links at Mottisfont (point 3) with the Horsebridge ride (route 15. point 2), which in turn links with the long and strenuous Stockbridge ride.

Refreshments

Romsey - Cobweb Tea Rooms, 49 The Hundred ☎ 01794 516434.
Latimer Coffee House, 11 Latimer Street ☎ 01794 513832.

Braishfield - Dog and Crook ☎ 01794 368530.
Newport Inn ☎ 01794 368225.

Mottisfont - Mottisfont Post Office Tea Rooms ☎ 01794 340243.

Dunbridge - Mill Arms ☎ 01794 340401.

Lockerley - Kings Arms ☎ 01794 340332.

Picnic - Mottisfont Abbey Gardens

*B*eginning from the small historic town of Romsey, this all-road ride explores some of the tiny undulating lanes that meander through and around the Test Valley. A few interesting villages along the route, plus the opportunity to visit Mottisfont Abbey Gardens (NT) beside the River Test, Broadlands and the impressive Abbey Church in Romsey.

START
Romsey. Located in the Test Valley on the A31, 10 miles (16km) south west of Winchester and 6 miles (10km) north of Southampton. Park in the main square or the Bus Station pay and display car park in Broadwater Road. OS grid ref: SU353210.

St Mary's church at Michelmersh.

ROUTE DIRECTIONS

1. From the town centre head north eastwards along the Winchester Road (A31), signposted Hursley and Winchester. Pass beneath the railway bridge and proceed for ¾ mile (1.2km) and turn left into Braishfield Road, signed to Hillier Gardens. At a crossroads turn right to visit the Gardens, otherwise keep ahead into Braishfield, passing the Dog and Crook and the Wheatsheaf before turning left into Newport Road, arrowed Michelmersh.

2. Pass the Newport Inn, then at a junction bear right and turn almost immediately left onto a narrow lane (not signposted). Ascend to a staggered crossroads and proceed straight on, the lane undulating into Michelmersh. Keep ahead at a crossroads along Haccups Road, then at a junction by The Elms, bear right to visit Michelmersh Church. Turn left for the main route, signed Mottisfont. At the next junction keep ahead, then turn left at a T-junction and descend to the A3057.

ALONG THE WAY

Romsey
An attractive market town with a famous 10th-century abbey which retains traces of its Saxon beginnings. The fine 18th-century house of Broadlands is set in a magnificent landscaped park beside the River Test and was once the home of Lord Mountbatten. Exhibitions and cafe. Open Easter to September ☎ 01794 516878.

St Mary's Church, Michelmersh
Perched high above the Test Valley, this fascinating church has an unusual detached and weatherboarded tower. Its timber-framed interior is thought to be 15th-century.

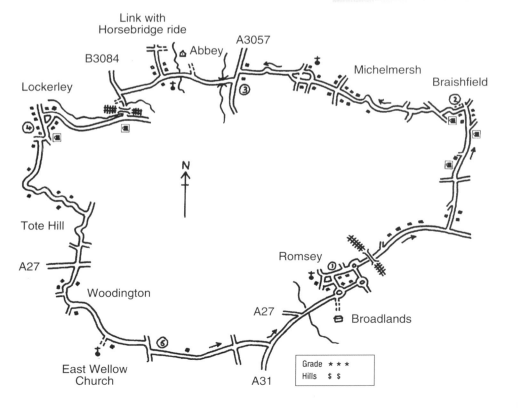

Grade ★ ★ ★
Hills $ $

Mottisfont Abbey Gardens (NT)
Set picturesquely beside the River Test, Mottisfont Abbey is an 18th-century house adapted from a 12th-century priory. The garden has splendid old trees and the famous walled rose garden is well worth a visit in June. Open April to October
☎ 01794 41220 & 40757.

St Margaret's Church, East Wellow
Set in a delightful rural setting and dating from the 13th-century, it has early 13th-century wall paintings and is the burial place of Florence Nightingale.

3. Turn left, then in 100 yards turn right towards Mottisfont and cross the River Test (link here with the Horsebridge ride). Pass the main entrance to Mottisfont Abbey Gardens and in the village bear left by the tea rooms to join a narrow lane leading to the B3084. Turn left downhill, cross the railway line and turn right in front of the Mill Arms for Lockerley. Cycle parallel with the River Dun, then keep left beside Lockerley village green to a T-junction.

4. Turn left, pass the Kings Arms, then shortly turn right and immediately left into Mount Lane by Lockerley Manor. Follow this winding and undulating narrow lane for 1½ miles (2.4km) through the hamlet of Tote Hill to a T-junction. Turn right and shortly reach the A27 Romsey to Salisbury road. Cross with care into Dandy's Ford Lane. Take the first turning left, signed Wellow Church. On reaching a T-junction, turn right, then in 200 yards bear left into Ryedown Lane, arrowed to Romsey.

5. Proceed for a mile (1.6km) to a staggered crossroads, go straight across and soon turn left onto the busy A31. Descend back into Romsey, passing the entrance to Broadlands and turn left at a roundabout back into the town centre.

RURAL LANES AROUND THE EAST HAMPSHIRE 'HANGERS' FROM SELBORNE

16½ miles (27km) / ¾ mile (1.2km) off-road

OS Map
Lamdranger 186 (Aldershot and Guildford) 1:50,000.

Nearest Railway Station
Liss, 1½ miles (2.4km) from point 5 near Hawkley.

Cycle Shops
Ransomes Cycles, Victoria Road, Alton ☎ 01420 82867.
Hampshire Cycle Centre, High Street, Alton ☎ 01420 82562.

Watchout!
- on the steep off-road descent through the Ashford Hanger Nature Reserve to the busy road throughSteep.
- generally on the narrow country lanes.

Refreshments

Selborne - Queens Hotel
☎ 01420 511454. Selborne Arms ☎ 01420 511247.
Tea Rooms.

Priors Dean - White Horse (Pub with No Mame) (character and real ale) ☎ 01420 588387.

Steep - Harrow Inn (character and hearty food)
☎ 01730 262685.

Hawkley - Hawkley Inn (real ales)
☎ 01730 284205.

A most pleasant ride, principally along quiet country lanes, around the beech hangers and hills in East Hampshire. A generally undulating route with two steep, strength-sapping hills and two short off-road sections. Allow plenty of time to complete the circuit, especially as it takes in three excellent pubs en route. Selborne village is also well worth exploring.

START

Selborne. Picturesque village located on the B3006, midway between Alton and Liss. Park in the National Trust car park situated behind the Selborne Arms pub. OS grid ref: SU742336.

ROUTE DIRECTIONS

1. Exit the car park, turn right along the B-road and leave the village. After ½ mile (0.8km) turn right, signed Newton Valence and climb a steep hill. Proceed along this lane for 2 miles (3.2km) towards East Tisted and take the left turn signposted Colemore and Priors Dean. Ascend steeply again, then take the first turning left (not signed).

2. Continue on this lane, arrowed Froxfield, and soon pass the White Horse pub, which is set back off the lane along a gravel track. At the crossroads, go straight across, then take the next left, opposite Claypits Lane. Proceed through a farmyard, bear right, then in 200 yards turn left and continue for ½ mile (0.8km) to a T-junction. Turn left, then shortly at a crossroads take the right turn for Froxfield Green and Langrish.

3. Continue to where the lane bears sharp right, just past the sign for Stoner Stables, and bear off left onto a track (entrance not immediately recognisable). Head steeply downhill through Ashford Hanger Nature Reserve. On reaching the road at the bottom, turn right, then immediately left, signed Ashford. Keep right beside

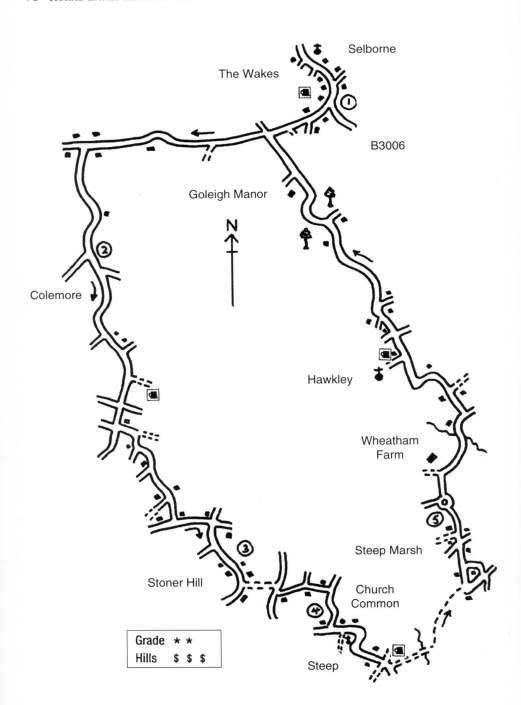

Byways House and continue downhill to a T-junction. Turn right up quite a steep hill to a further T-junction in Steep village, just past the War Memorial.

4. Turn left, passing Bedales School and the parish church and proceed downhill, soon to turn left to the Harrow Inn and refreshment. Follow the track past the pub, cross a stream and pass beside cottages into woodland. Shortly, on reaching a lane, turn left and keep left at the next junction. Stay on this lane, bearing left towards Oakshott and Wheatham and soon pass JK Engineering and the Brickyards. Tackle a steep incline and bear right at the top, signed Wheatham.

5 Keep right, arrowed Hawkley, and. pass Wheatham Farm on your left. Proceed to a T-junction and turn left for Hawkley and continue along this lane in the direction of Empshott. By turning left at the next junction you will reach the attractive village of Hawkley and a useful refreshment stop, the Hawkley Inn. Otherwise, keep ahead towards Newton Valence and climb a steep hill with Goleigh Manor at the top. Remain on this lane to a T-junction and turn right to rejoin your outward route back into Selborne.

The rustic and unspoilt Harrow Inn at Steep.

LANES, VILLAGES AND BYWAYS FROM THE ROMAN TOWN AT SILCHESTER

20 miles (32km) / 3½ miles (5.6km) off-road

OS Maps
Landranger 175 (Reading and Windsor)
and 174 (Newbury and Wantage)
1:50,000.

Nearest Railway Station
Bramley (on the route at point 5).

Cycle Shops/Hire
Mountain Movers (hire), Weighmore
House, Crockford Lane, Chineham, 2½
miles (4km) east of Sherborne St John
☎ 01256 814138.
Winklebury Cycles (hire) Winklebury
Centre, Basingstoke
☎ 01256 20645 & 331444.
Raleigh Cycle Centre, 22 Winchester
Street, Basingstoke ☎ 01256 465266.

Watchout!
- when crossing the busy A340 (twice).

Link Information
An extended tour of North Hampshire
can be acheived by linking with the
Kingsclere ride (route 17, point 3) and
the Wellington Country Park ride
(route 28, point 2).

Refreshments

Silchester - Calleva Arms (Gales
ales) ☎ 01734 700305.
Little London - Plough
☎ 01256 850628.
Charter Alley - White Hart (range
of real ales) ☎ 01256 850048.
Monk Sherborne - Mole Inn
☎ 01256 850033.
Sherborne St John - Swan
☎ 01256 8501 0165. The Vyne
(NT) - lunches and teas
☎ 01256 881337.
Stratfield Saye - New Inn ☎ 01734
332255. Stratfield Saye House Tea
Room ☎ 01256 882882.

*A*n easy and enjoyable tour around the gently undulating lanes
and byways north of Basingstoke. Interesting diversions along
the way include the fascinating Roman site of Calleva with its small
museum, several attractive villages, Stratfield Saye House and the
Vyne, a beautiful Tudor country house with gardens and woodland
walks (National Trust). One short stretch of off-road bridleway can be
very muddy after prolonged rain. This ride links with both route 17
and 28, creating an extensive tour of North Hampshire.

START

Roman site at Silchester. Located 4 miles (6.4km) off the
A340 Basingstoke to Tadley road (signposted). Good
parking outside St Mary the Virgin church, situated just
inside the Roman walls 1½ miles (2.4km) east of the
village. OS grid ref: SU643624.

ROUTE DIRECTIONS

1. From the parking area turn left along the lane and take
the arrowed bridleway on your left. If wishing to visit the
Roman amphitheatre continue along the lane to the
sharp left-hand bend and go through the kissing gate
opposite. Back on the bridleway, follow the gravel track
beside the Old Manor and barn on staddle stones to a
gate, then bear left along a wide fenced trackway which
cuts across the centre of the walled Roman town. On
reaching the perimeter wall, turn left alongside the wall,
then shortly bear right through a gate and reach a further
gate near cottages. Continue along a pitted track to a
lane near the small museum.

2. Cross straight over onto a short stretch of old track,
then turn left along a lane into Silchester. Keep to this
undulating lane for nearly 2 miles (3.2km), passing
through Little London, to reach a T-junction and turn
right along Bramley Road, signed Basingstoke. In ½ mile
(0.8km) turn right onto the A340, then immediately left
into Ramsdell Road, signposted Charter Alley.

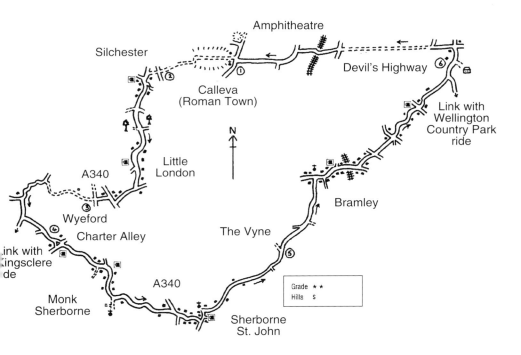

Amphitheatre
Silchester
Devil's Highway
Calleva
(Roman Town)
Link with
Wellington
Country Park
ride
N
Little
London
A340
Bramley
Wyeford
Charter Alley
The Vyne
Link with
Kingsclere
de
A340
Monk
Sherborne
Sherborne
St. John

Grade ★ ★
Hills   S

3. At a sharp left-hand bend, just beyond Pamber Place Cottage, keep ahead along a private gravel drive towards 'Wyeford'. Follow the drive for ½ mile (0.8km) and pass between the fine moated brick house and outbuildings, then bear right and left along a bridleway through woodland (can be muddy) to a gate. Bear right for 250 yards to a lane and turn left. At a T-junction, turn left (unsigned) downhill and take the first left towards Monk Sherborne. (Keep ahead if wishing to link with the Kingsclere Ride).

4. Enter Charter Alley, passing the White Hart, then keep left at a T-junction and follow a gently undulating lane for a mile (1.6km) into Monk Sherborne. Continue through the village, signed Sherborne St John, keeping left at the war memorial and soon arrive at the A340. Taking great care, turn right, then shortly bear off left along Cranes Road into Sherborne St John. Turn left at a T-junction and proceed through the village and in 1½ miles (2.4km) pass the entrance to The Vyne (NT).

ALONG THE WAY

The Vyne, Sherborne St John
Bequeathed to the National Trust in 1956 by the Chute family, this fine brick-built house dates back to the time of Henry VIII. Much of the exterior is 16th-century, but several alterations over the years include the interesting addition of the earliest classical portico on an English country house. Inside, there is a fascinating Tudor chapel, a Palladian staircase and a wealth of panelling and fine furniture. Lake, grounds and walks. Open April to September. ☎ 01256 881337.

5. Remain on this level lane for a further 1½ miles (2.4km) to a T-junction and turn right into Bramley. Cross the railway line and turn immediately left into Bramley Lane, signposted Stratfield Saye. In a mile (1.6km), keep ahead at a crossroads and proceed for another mile (1.6km) to a staggered crossroads just beyond the New Inn. Go straight across and soon pass a lane on your right leading to the entrance to Stratfield Saye House. (Take this lane if wishing to incorporate the Wellington Country Park ride).

The Vyne (NT) near Sherborne St John.

6. Pass Home Farm, then at a staggered crossroads (unsigned) turn left and in 200 yards, where the lane bears sharp right, veer off left onto an arrowed bridleway, known as the Devil's Highway (Roman Road). Follow this generally good surfaced track for 1½ miles (2.4km) to a junction of lanes and go straight on. Cross the railway, then at a T-junction turn left and soon follow the lane right, signed Silchester, to reach a T-junction close to Silchester church. Turn left back to your car.

Silchester

The Roman town of 'Calleva Atrebatum' developed after the Roman invasion in 43 AD and grew into a large prosperous settlement. For reasons unknown, the town suffered a gradual decline in the 5th century AD. It was thoroughly excavated between 1890 and 1909 exposing the most complete plan of any provincial town in the Roman Empire, including a road network, foundations of buildings and defensive works. The 1½ miles (2.4km) of encircling walls are in good condition, but they now enclose agricultural land. Many of the treasures unearthed during the excavations are housed in Reading Museum, although the tiny Calleva Museum houses a pictorial display of the history of the town. ☎ 01734 700450. The 9,000-seat amphitheatre is also worth a visit.

Bramley

Much expanded commuter village with a most interesting parish church. St James's church boasts one of the best-furnished interiors in the county, including a fine gallery dating from 1735, a 15th-century screen, splendid old stained glass, wall paintings and ancient bench-ends.

Stratfield Saye House

The magnificent home of the Dukes of Wellington, built in 1630 and given by the nation to the first Duke in 1817, after his victory over Napoleon at the Battle of Waterloo. It contains a fine collection of furniture, paintings and various mementoes of the 1st Duke. ☎ 01256 882882.

ROUTE 26

PEACEFUL VALLEY VILLAGES AND OPEN DOWNLAND TRACKS FROM STOCKBRIDGE

26 miles (42km) / 8½ miles (13.6km) off-road

OS Maps
Landranger 185 (Winchester and Basingstoke) and 184 (Salisbury and The Plain) 1:50,000.

Nearest Railway Station
Andover, 2 miles (2.4km.) from point 3 on the ride.

Cycle Shops
1 Track Cycles, Love Lane, Andover
☎ 01264 332986.
Andover Bicycle Centre, Union Street,
Andover ☎ 01264 352046.
Les Smith Cycles, Weyhill Road,
Andover ☎ 01264 352991.

Watchout!
- on the short stretches of fast A-road.
- some blind corners on the narrow lanes.
- a few bumpy descents on rutted tracks.
- for the very steep climb up Whiteshoot Hill onto Broughton Down - save some energy for this gruelling climb!

Link Information
Explore the Test Way and Valley further by linking with the Horsebridge ride (route 15, point 8), which in turn links with the Romsey ride (route 23).

*T*his ride is not only one of the longest, but it incorporates some of the most challenging downland tracks on the Wiltshire/ Hampshire border, especially the strength-sapping climb up Broughton Down. An interesting combination of the Test Way, country lanes and generally good surfaced tracks across chalk downland with splendid views. The ride explores a few of the most picturesque villages in the area. Allow plenty of time to complete this circuit.

START

Stockbridge. Country village situated on the A30 between Winchester and Salisbury in the Test Valley. Parking spaces along the length of the High Street. OS grid ref: SU355351.

ROUTE DIRECTIONS

1. Head eastwards along the High Street and bear left at the roundabout along the A30. Keep left at the next roundabout to join the A3057 towards Andover, then after 100 yards bear off left to join the waymarked Test Way, which follows the course of the old railway. Shortly, pass beside a wooden barrier and keep to a defined path parallel with the A-road for 2 miles (3.2km) to where the Test Way goes beneath the A3057 near the Mayfly pub.

2. Immediately bear off right to a lane, opposite West Down car park. Turn right, then right again along the A-road and cross the bridge over the River Test. In ¼ mile (0.4km), take the left turn signposted Longstock and cross the River Anton. Keep right at the next junction and climb steadily out of the valley to a trig point at the top. Proceed to a crossroads, turn right and descend into Goodworth Clatford, passing the Clatford Arms.

3. Continue through the Anton Valley on this good level road via Upper Clatford and Anna Valley to reach the A343, just south of Andover. Turn left, then in 150 yards

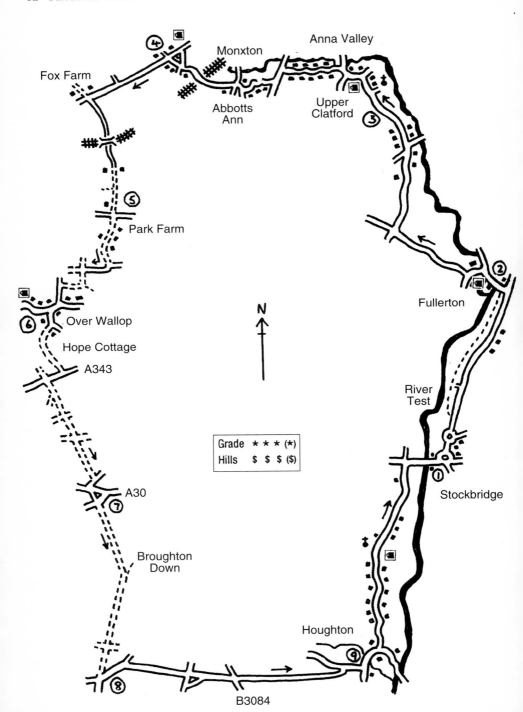

Refreshments

Stockbridge - four pubs, a café and tea room.

Testcombe - The Mayfly (excellent riverside garden, food all day) ☎ 01264 860283.

Upper Clatford - Crook and Shears ☎ 01264 361543.

Abbots Ann - Popular Farm Inn (open all day) ☎ 01264 710649. Eagle ☎ 01264 710339.

Monxton - Black Swan ☎ 01264 710260.

Over Wallop - White Hart ☎ 01264 781331.

Houghton - The Boot ☎ 01794 388310.

Picturesque Fullerton Mill set astride the River Anton.

turn right by the Poplar Farm Inn for Little Ann. Cycle round a series of sharp bends and enter Abbots Ann. At a T-junction turn right, then soon bear left, signposted Monxton, and follow this narrow lane into the delightful thatched village of Monxton.

4. Turn left into Green Lane at the crossroads, signed Quarley, and proceed for 1½ miles (2.4km) to a crossroads by a telephone box. Turn left up a dead-end lane, pass beneath a railway bridge, then soon leave the tarmac just beyond the entrance to Georgia Farm. Follow a rutted grass track, ignore the arrowed bridleway right near a house, and continue on a narrow path through scrub to reach a wide track by Oklahoma Farm. At a road, turn right, then immediately left onto a waymarked track and pass through Park Farm.

5. Track soon gives way to tarmac, then at a lane opposite a large barn, turn right and in ¼ mile (0.4km) at a crossing of paths by the sign to Wallop Farm, follow the arrowed Right of Way left through trees. At a T-junction of tracks, turn right, then left at the next junction and descend into Over Wallop. Bear right by the War Memorial, then turn left over the Wallop Brook into Salisbury Lane.

Along the Way

Stockbridge
Attractive one-street country town stretching across the idyllic Test Valley. A popular destination for fishermen in search of trout in the Test, one of the most sought-after game rivers in the country.

Test Way
This long distance footpath traverses Hampshire from south to north, a distance of 46 miles (73km), and for two-thirds of its length it follows the valley of the River Test. Ten miles (16km) of the valley route are along the disused Test Valley Railway, once affectionately known as the 'Sprat and Winkle ' line.

Over Wallop

One of three picturesque and peaceful villages that nestle beside the willowed Wallop Brook, which meanders lazily through Broughton to merge with the River Test. An enchanting collection of thatched and cob cottages cluster around the church of St Peter in Over Wallop, which has a fine 15th-century font.

Broughton Down

Steep downland with beech woods, ancient droveways, tumuli and stunning views. There is a nature reserve on the top which preserves the plants, grasses and flowers - cowslips, rock rose, various orchids - that favour the rich chalk grasslands that have rapidly disappeared through intensive modern agriculture.

Houghton

A straggling Test Valley village, lined with an assortment of thatched, brick and timber-framed houses. Of note, are the red-brick vicarage and Manor House and All Saints church, which has a 19th-century spire and shingled tower. Houghton Lodge is an 18th-century fishing lodge on the Test, boasting some fine riverside and walled gardens (open to the public.)

6. Climb uphill, bearing left, then turn right onto a farm track in front of Hope Cottage. Keep left at a fork by an old corrugated barn and gradually ascend on a good grassy track across fields to the A343. Turn right, then in 100 yards, bear off left at a crossing of tracks. Just beyond a bungalow keep straight on at a fork and descend on the wide hedged track, disregarding all left and right turns. Rise and dip for the next mile (1.6km) to a lane, turn right, then left along the A30 for a short distance and turn right, signposted West Tytherley.

7. Ascend, then at a sharp right-hand bend keep ahead onto a good track and descend steadily, before beginning a long and arduous climb up Broughton Down. Pause for a breather at the top and enjoy the far-reaching views. Pass Broughton Down Nature Reserve and undulate on the excellent trackway to a crossing of paths and the Clarendon Way. Keep straight across and descend to a lane.

8. Turn left uphill, then in ½ mile (0.8km), go across an unmarked crossroads. Shortly, bear left at the next junction, then cross the B3084 at a staggered junction and follow the ridge road with splendid views into the valley of the Wallop Brook and over Broughton. Descend to a T-junction, turn right, then soon bear left at the junction in the Test Valley at Bossington.

9. After ¼ mile (0.4km) enter Houghton and turn next left, signposted Stockbridge. Proceed through the village and along the valley for 2½ miles (4km) to the A30 at Stockbridge and turn right back to your car.

THROUGH THE 'HAMPSHIRE HIGHLANDS' FROM WALBURY HILL

15 miles (24km) / 5½ miles (8.8km) off-road

OS Map
Landranger 174 (Newbury and Wantage) 1:50,000.

Nearest Railway Station
Kintbury (Berkshire), 4 miles (7.4km) north of walbury Hill.

Cycle Shop/Hire
Craven Cycles, 40 Bartholomew Street, Newbury ☎ 01635 582872. Rentalle (hire), Newbury ☎ 01635 31276. The Cycle Shop, Cheap Street, Newbury ☎ 01635 582100.

Watchout!
- along the rutted and often muddy ridge track.
- on the dificult track descent into Netherton.

Link Information
An extended ride through this picturesque part of North Hampshire can be achieved by joining the Hurstbourne Tarrant ride (route 16, point 5).

Refreshments

Vernham Dean - George Inn (excellent garden/good value pub food) ☎ 01264 87279.

Upton - Crown (children not permitted) ☎ 01264 76265.

Faccombe - Jack Russell (garden/children welcome) ☎ 01264 87315.

A short and quite energetic ride through the delightfully rural 'Hampshire Highlands', an area of rolling hills and combes located in the far north eastern corner of the county. The route encompasses some of the tiny, traffic-free lanes that criss-cross the area and the exhilarating ridge-top track that traverses Walbury, Inkpen and Ham Hills, which affords magnificent far-reaching views into Berkshire and Wiltshire. Not a ride to rush, and if wishing to explore the area further, this route links with the Bourne Valley ride.

START
Walbury Hill. Free parking area located at the top of the hill and best approached from the A343 Andover to Newbury road. Follow a lane signposted to Faccombe, just north of Hurstbourne Tarrant, for a 5 mile (8km) drive, via Faccombe, to reach Walbury Hill.
OS grid ref: SU379616.

ROUTE DIRECTIONS
1. From the parking area on top of Walbury Hill take the good ridge track westwards (Wayfarer's Walk) and gently ascend to pass through the just visible earth ramparts of Walbury Hill-fort. With magnificent far-reaching views north across Berkshire and Wiltshire, descend to a parking area and lane. Cross straight over and climb onto Inkpen Hill, passing the macabre Combe Gibbet. Remain on this ridge-top track, which has sadly been severely rutted by excessive 4-wheel drive vehicle activity, for 2 miles (3.2km) to reach a lane.

2. Turn right, then left at the T-junction signposted Fosbury. Initially climb, then enjoy a welcome freewheel downhill for ¾ mile (1.2km), before turning left, signed Henley. Follow the tiny valley bottom lane into the charming thatched hamlet, then ascend steadily to a T-junction and turn right towards Vernham Dean. Again

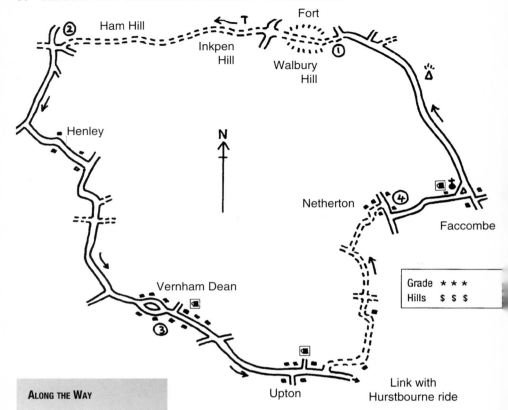

Grade ★ ★ ★
Hills $ $ $

ALONG THE WAY

Walbury Hill

The highest chalk hill in England at 959ft with the obvious remains of a hill-fort or camp crowning its summit. The single rampart and ditch is a mile long and encloses 82 acres of land.

Inkpen Hill

The beginning of the Wayfarers Walk long-distance trail which traverses Hampshire to Emsworth, a total of 70 miles. At the highest point, on Gallows Down, is an impressive Neolithic long barrow, 6ft high and 200ft long. Perched on top is the Combe Gibbet, a grisly landmark that was first

descend on an excellent rural lane for 1½ miles (2.4km) to a T-junction and turn left (unsigned) shortly to enter Vernham Dean. Bear left along Back Lane, soon to rejoin the main valley road at the George Inn.

3. Continue through the village and along the level valley bottom road for 1½ miles (2.4km) into Upton. Keep ahead at the crossroads, then in 20 yards, turn left onto a track, beside a wall and gates to a house, (continue along the lane to link with the Hurstbourne Tarrant ride) and soon bear right through the valley. Shortly, veer sharp left to climb steadily uphill on a good stony track out of the valley. Bear left, then right by a farm building and proceed straight on at a crossing of tracks to briefly join the Test Way. At a junction, take the arrowed Right of Way right and follow an earth track (can be muddy), keeping left at a fork to begin a steady descent (could be tricky) into the remote hamlet of Netherton.

The 17th-century George Inn at Vernham Dean.

4. On reaching a T-junction with a lane turn right, then next left, signed Faccombe with a fine thatched barn to your left. Begin a long ascent, necessitating regular gear-changing as it steepens and eventually enter the estate village of Faccombe. Pass the Jack Russell pub, a welcome refreshment spot, and turn left, signed East Woodhay. Pass the church and gently climb with stunning North Hampshire views towards a transmitting mast on Combe Hill. Shortly, descend quickly with vistas across the Berkshire Vale and bear left back to the car park at Walbury Hill.

erected in 1676 to hang a local man accused of murder.

Vernham Dean
Tranquil village tucked away in a valley close to the Wiltshire border and the delightfully remote and unspoilt rolling landscape of the North Wessex Downs.

Faccombe
Classic estate village, complete with village pond, centred around a large Georgian manor house and surrounded by rolling downland and splendid views. It is the most northerly village in the county and is only 3 metres short of being the highest village, this accolade going to its near neighbour Ashmansworth.

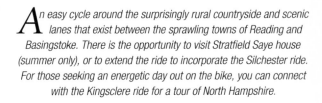

ROUTE 28

NORTH HAMPSHIRE LANES AROUND WELLINGTON COUNTRY PARK

16 miles (26km) all road

OS Map
Landranger 175 (Reading and Windsor)
1:50,000.

Nearest Railway Station
Mortimer, 3½ miles (5.6km) west.

Cycle Shops/Hire
Mountain Movers (hire), Weighmore
House, Crockford Lane, Chineham
☎ 01256 814138. Raleigh Cycle
Centre, 22 Winchester Street,
Basingstoke ☎ 01256 465266.
Winklebury Cycles (hire), Winklebury
Centre, Basingstoke
☎ 01256 20645 & 331444.

Watchout!
- when crossing all the A-roads as they
are fast and busy.
- on the blind bends along the narrow
lanes.

Link Information
This route links with the Silchester ride
(route 26, point 6), which in turn
connects with the Kingsclere circuit
(route 17, point 3), giving the opportunity for an extensive and energetic tour
of North Hampshire.

An easy cycle around the surprisingly rural countryside and scenic lanes that exist between the sprawling towns of Reading and Basingstoke. There is the opportunity to visit Stratfield Saye house (summer only), or to extend the ride to incorporate the Silchester ride. For those seeking an energetic day out on the bike, you can connect with the Kingsclere ride for a tour of North Hampshire.

START

Wellington Country Park. Recreation area signposted off the A33 Reading to Basingstoke road, 7 miles (11.2km) north of Basingstoke. Country Park car park open daily mid February to October and winter weekends only. Alternatively, park at Riseley Memorial Hall, 200 yards north of the roundabout at the Country Park entrance. OS grid ref: SU726628.

ROUTE DIRECTIONS

1. Leave the Country Park entrance and take the second exit off the roundabout towards Reading and the A33. Continue ahead at the next roundabout (busy A33-take care), signposted Beech Hill and Stratfield Saye. Shortly, cross the River Loddon and follow the edge of Stratfield Saye Park to reach a staggered crossroads. (Proceed straight ahead to join the Silchester ride).

2. Turn left signed Bramley, pass Home Farm, then in ¼ mile (0.4km) bear off left beside the Park and soon pass the entrance to Stratfield Saye House (open to public). Bear left with the lane around the perimeter of the Park and after ½ mile (0.8km) reach the A33 and the Wellington Arms. Cross straight over, arrowed Mattingley, to join a quiet narrow lane that twists and curves, passing Daneshill School, to reach a T-junction. Turn right into the hamlet of Turgis Green.

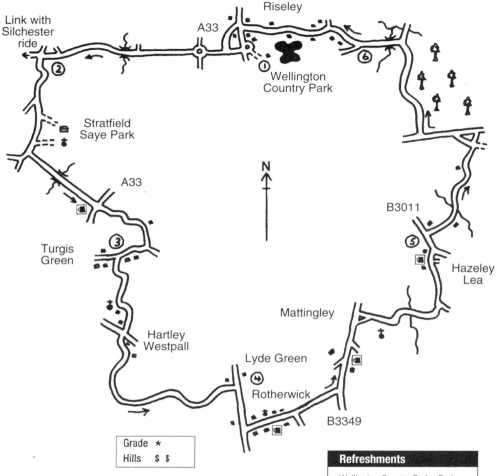

Grade ★
Hills $ $

3. Take the next lane left for Hartley Westpall and soon pass the isolated farm and attractive church, before reaching a T-junction on the edge of the village. Turn left, then almost immediately right along the village street, soon to pass a fine mill straddling the River Loddon. Continue for a mile (1.6km) to a T-junction beside the Fox at Lyde Green.

4. Turn right into Rotherwick, then in ¼ mile (0.4km), turn left arrowed Mattingley and follow the picturesque village street, passing the church and the Coach and Horses. Keep to this lane for ¾ mile (1.2km) to the B3349. Turn left and take great care on this often busy

Refreshments

Wellington Country Park - Park café.

Stratfield Saye House - Tea Room (if visiting house).

Stratfield Turgis - Wellington Arms (upmarket hotel, good bar food) ☎ 01256 882214.

Lyde Green - Fox (locals' pub) ☎ 01256 882279.

Rotherwick - Coach and Horses (open all day, excellent range of real ale)☎ 01256 762542. Falcon ☎ 01256 762586.

Mattingley - Leather Bottle ☎ 01734 326371.

ALONG THE WAY

Wellington Country Park
Covering some 350 acres, this popular recreation area offers visitors a Nature Trail through woodland and boating, windsurfing and canoeing on a large lake. Other attractions include a dairy industry museum, a children's animal farm, a miniature steam railway, an adventure playground and camping and caravanning facilities. Admission charge.
☎ 01734 326444.

Stratfield Saye House
The magnificent home of the Dukes of Wellington, built in 1630 and given by the nation to the first Duke in 1817, after his victory over Napoleon at the Battle of Waterloo. It contains a fine collection of furniture, paintings and various mementoes of the 1st Duke, including his splendid funeral carriage. Special events.
☎ 01256 882882.

St Mary's Church, Hartley Westpall
Dating from the 14th-century and restored in 1868, this attractive isolated church is notable for the original woodwork - roof-beams, supporting pillars, doorways - and the unique, half-timbered 14th-century west wall. Jacobean pulpit.

Mattingley Church
Another fine church on the route that is well worth a closer look. It is remarkable for its unusual construction; the walls are timber-framed throughout with the infilling between the timbers being of brick-nogging.

Duke of Wellington's monument at Stratfield Saye.

road into Mattingley. Pass the Leather Bottle pub, then take the second turning right towards Mattingley Church and Hazeley. Keep right at a T-junction, pass the church access lane and proceed on this undulating road to the B3011 at Hazeley Lea.

5. Bear left, then immediately right towards Hazeley Lea and shortly cross the River Whitewater. Steadily climb on this lane and enter Bramshill. At a crossroads (police college to your right), turn left for Heckfield, then at the T-junction ahead, keep left beside Bramshill Plantation. After ½ mile (0.8km) turn right at the end of the trees into Ford Lane. Continue past Well House Lane and soon bear sharp left (ford ahead) to cross the river bridge.

6. Shortly, pass a riding stables, then at a T-junction turn left, signposted Riseley. Proceed for ½ mile (0.8km) into the village centre and turn left at the T-junction, passing the Memorial Hall to reach a roundabout and the entrance to Wellington Country Park.

IN AND AROUND THE INFANT TEST VALLEY FROM WHITCHURCH

19½ miles (31km) / 6 miles (10km) off-road

OS Map
Landranger 185 (Winchester and Basingstoke) 1:50,000.

Nearest Railway Station
Whitchurch.

Cycle Shop/Hire
Test Valley Sports and Cycles, Whitchurch ☎ 01256 893778.
Intrepid Trips (Hire & Spares), Freefolk, nr Whitchurch ☎ 01256 893432.

Watchout!
- when crossing the busy A34 at Tufton Warren.
- on the busy lanes close to the A303 intersection near Micheldever Station.
- on what can be a very muddy and slippery off-road section (Harrow Way) north of Overton, especially in winter.

Whitchurch Silk Mill and the River Test.

*T*his undulating ride explores the downland tracks and scenic country lanes near the infant River Test, which rises just east of Overton. Some tracks can be very wet, muddy and slippery after prolonged rain.

Refreshments

Whitchurch - Silk Mill Café
☎ 01256 893882,
White Hart ☎ 01256 892900,
Old Brewery ☎ 01256 892145,
Kings Arms ☎ 01256 893489

Overton - Greyhound
☎ 01256 770241
White Hart (open all day Saturday) ☎ 01256 770237

START

Whitchurch. Free car park beside Whitchurch Silk Mill on the Winchester Road. Village is located on the B3400, 6 miles (10km) east of Andover and ½ mile (0.8km) off the A34 Winchester to Newbury road.
OS grid ref: SU463479.

ROUTE DIRECTIONS

1. From the car park turn right along the Winchester Road towards the A34. Leave the village, keep right beneath the A34 and follow the route right into a narrow lane and Tufton. Follow the single track road uphill, then descend and keep straight on for Longparish where the lane veers sharp right towards Hurstbourne Priors. Proceed for a mile (1.6km) parallel with the River Test to a track and postbox on your left.

2. Turn left, gradually pedal uphill past a house and beneath an old railway bridge on a good track, then at a T-junction of routes, follow the main grass-centred track left, eventually reaching the A34 beyond Firgo Farm.

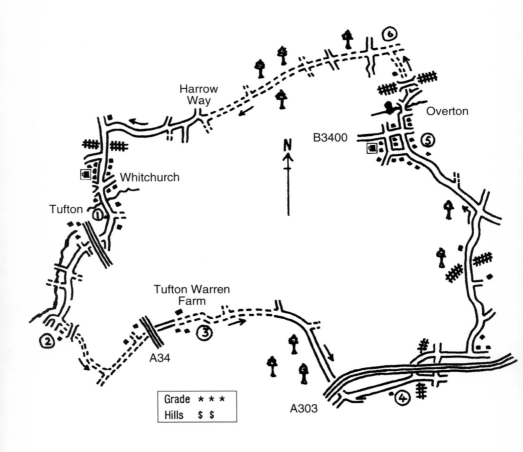

Taking great care cross the dual carriageway onto a metalled farm road, signposted Tufton Warren, and pass through the farmyard. Note the unusual thatched clocktower.

3. Beyond the barns join a wide grassy bridleway. Bear right, then left at a fork, following the defined track alongside a field. After nearly a mile (1.6km), bear right at a lane and shortly pass the entrance to Roundwood Estate. Go under the busy A303, then at a T-junction turn left for Micheldever Station. Ignore the right turn for the station, keep ahead for ½ mile (0.8km) and turn right at the T-junction close to the A303 and descend to a further T-junction.

4. Turn left beneath the A303, then turn right signed Popham and take the next lane left, arrowed Steventon and Deane. Head north on this delightful lane, passing tumuli in the field on your left, and continue with fine views across the Test Valley to a fork of roads. Keep straight on, signposted Overton, for 2 miles (3.2km) to an unsigned crossroads. Turn left and descend through woodland into Overton.

5. Bear left into Pound Road, then shortly at a T-junction, turn right down the main street into the village centre. At the traffic lights and B3400, turn right, then almost immediately go left into Station Road. Cross the River Test, pass the Station access road and gently climb following signs to Portals and Overton Mill. Pass beneath the railway bridge, bear right, then left onto a grass-centred track between the Mill and car park. Head uphill, then undulate on the wide track to a T-junction.

6. Turn left, then after 100 yards cross the B3051 onto an arrowed Right of Way - the Harrow Way. Continue along this ridge-top track which can be exceedingly muddy and slippery after wet weather. Ignore all side routes and after 2 miles (3.2km) reach a metalled lane. Go straight across, merge left with a further lane and follow this undulating road to a T-junction. Turn left and shortly descend into the centre of Whitchurch and the car park.

River Test
One of the finest chalk streams in Europe and famous for its excellent trout fishing. It rises near Overton and flows peacefully south through scenic countryside to the Solent.

Portals (Overton Mill)
The iron-free water of the Test is ideal for paper-making. Henri Portal established a paper-making mill on the river in 1712 and still produces watermarked paper for the Bank of England. Originally based at Laverstoke along the river, it moved to Overton in 1950.

MEON VALLEY RAILWAY PATH AND PEACEFUL LANES FROM WICKHAM

16 miles (25.7km) / 3½ miles (5.6km) off-road

OS Maps
Landranger 196 (Solent and the Isle of Wight) and 185 (Winchester and Basingstoke) 1:50,000.

Nearest Railway Station
Fareham, 3 miles (4.8km) south.

Cycle Shops/Hire
Bikes at Botley (repairs/hire/mobile workshop), 22 Winchester Street, Botley, 5 miles (8km west)
☎ 01489 790980.

Watchout!
- for mud and water on the old railway path in winter.
- steep descent to the B-road in Hambledon.
- steep ascent out of Hambledon.
- along the 4 mile (6.4km) stretch of the B2177 to Wickham

Link Information
Where this route leaves the old railway path near Soberton it links with the Bishops Waltham ride (route 10, point 5).

A not-too-energetic cycle along a section of the disused Meon Valley railway line, and along a network of quiet narrow lanes, via the picturesque villages of Hambledon and Southwick. Gently undulating terrain, except for one steep climb out of Hambledon.

START
Wickham. Attractive village located just off the A32 Alton to Fareham road, 3½ miles (5.6km) north of Fareham. Free car park and good parking in the main square. OS grid ref: SU573115.

Refreshments
Wickham - various pubs and a tea room.
Soberton - White Lion ☎ 01489 877346.
Hambledon - Vine ☎ 01705 632419. George Hotel (no food Monday) ☎ 01705 632318. Lotts Tea Room
Worlds End - Chairmaker's Arms ☎ 01705 255990.
Southwick - Golden Lion ☎ 01705 379134.

ROUTE DIRECTIONS
1. From the village square head away from the A334, passing the Old House Hotel on your right, and shortly bear right downhill to pass beneath the old railway bridge to the junction with the A32. Just beyond the bridge climb the few wooden steps up onto the disused Meon Valley Railway line. Turn right and follow this delightful route northwards for just over 4 miles (6.4km). Pass beneath five bridges, then on reaching the sixth bridge, climb the steps on your right onto a lane and follow it right into Soberton. (Turn left to incorporate the Bishops Waltham ride).

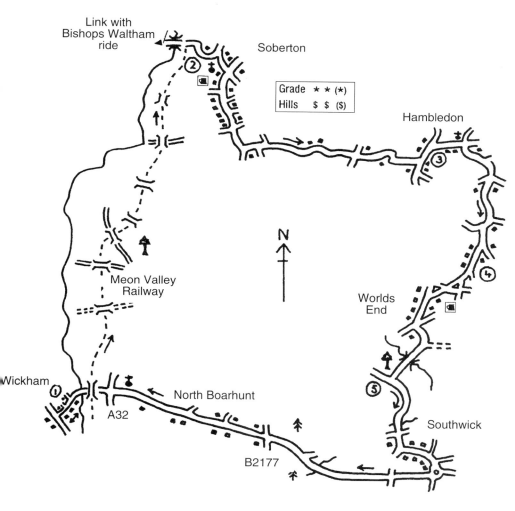

2. Pass the church and green, turn right and head downhill past the White Lion to a crossroads. Turn right, signposted Soberton Heath, then keep left by the war memorial and descend to a junction on your left, signposted Hoe Cross and Hambledon. Keep right at the next junction, then proceed ahead at the crossroads at Hoe Cross and soon descend steeply to the B2150 in Hambledon.

3. Turn left by Lotts Tea Room and turn right in 200 yards, signed Clanfield into the village centre. Shortly,

Opposite: Peaceful traffic-free cycling along the disused Meon Valley railway line.

ALONG THE WAY

Wickham
William of Wykeham was born at this attractive Meon-Valley town in 1324 and later founded both Winchester College and New College in Oxford. Pleasant Georgian houses surround a wide square and add a characteristic touch of elegance to the area.

Meon Valley Railway
Delightful 14 mile (22.4km) stretch of old railway line linking Wickham to West Meon. Now a popular bridleway that explores the picturesque Meon Valley.

Soberton
A peaceful village set close to the River Meon and on the Wayfarer's Walk. Demons and gargoyles decorate the tower of the 16th-century church, which also has wall-paintings and a rare 17th-century altar cloth.

Southwick
'The D-Day Village' is an estate village. Southwick House, still occupied by the Navy, was Eisenhower's headquarters for the D-Day invasion. The old part of the village has changed little over the years with timber-framed cottages, 18th-century brick houses and a tiny green with a pump. The church of St James was rebuilt in 1566 and is a rare example of a post-Reformation Tudor church. The Golden Lion pub brewed its own beer between 1800 and 1956. The machinery has been restored to working order and the brewhouse is open by appointment.

An attractive village shop façade.

turn right beside the George Hotel and climb steeply out of the village to pass Rushmere Pond. After a mile (1.6km), bear left onto the B2150, then in 100 yards turn right into Uplands Road and head for Worlds End.

4. Proceed ahead at a crossroads, then at a T-junction turn left, passing Willow Lakes Fisheries. In ½ mile (0.8km) turn left beside the Chairmaker's pub and almost immediately bear off right into Apless Lane. Keep to this quiet narrow lane passing Creech Wood and across Beckford Bridge to reach a T-junction.

5. Turn left (not signed), and gently descend into Southwick. At the next junction, bear left and soon follow the lane left into the picturesque village, bearing right in front of the church. Keep right at the further junction (entrance to HMS Dryad to the left) and shortly reach a roundabout. Follow the B2177 right, signposted Wickham, and remain on this road for 4 miles (6.4km) back to the A32. Proceed straight across into the village centre and your car.